C000026549

Leading the Leaders
for the Future

Also available from Network Continuum

Nurturing Independent Thinkers
Mike Bosher and Patrick Hazlewood

Learn to Transform
David Crossley and Graham Corbyn

Regenerating Schools
Malcolm Groves

Distributing Leadership for Personalizing Learning
Ron Ritchie and Ruth Deakin Crick

Leading the Leaders for the Future

A Transformational Opportunity

Mike Bosher and Patrick Hazlewood OxFORD

continuum

Continuum International Publishing Group
Network Continuum

The Tower Building	80 Maiden Lane
11 York Road	Suite 704
London, SE1 7NX	New York, NY 10038

www.networkcontinuum.co.uk
www.continuumbooks.com

© Mike Bosher and Patrick Hazlewood 2008

All rights reserved. No part of this publication may be reproduced or transmitted in any form or by any means, electronic or mechanical, including photocopying, recording, or any information storage or retrieval system, without prior permission in writing from the publishers.

Mike Bosher and Patrick Hazlewood 2008 have asserted their rights under the Copyright, Designs and Patents Act, 1988, to be identified as Authors of this work.

British Library Cataloguing-in-Publication Data
A catalogue record for this book is available from the British Library.

ISBN: 9781855394773 (paperback)

Library of Congress Cataloging-in-Publication Data
Bosher, Mike.
Leading the leaders for the future : a transformational opportunity /
Mike Bosher and Patrick Hazlewood.
    p. cm.
Includes bibliographical references.
ISBN: 978-1-85539-477-3 (pbk.)
1. Educational leadership–Great Britain. 2. School management and organization–
Great Britain. 3. School improvement programs–Great Britain. 4. Education–
Curricula–Great Britain. I. Hazlewood, Patrick. II. Title.

LB2900.5.B67 2008
371.200941—dc22

                                                              2008051172

Typeset by Newgen Imaging Systems Pvt Ltd, Chennai, India
Printed and bound in Great Britain by CPI Antony Rowe, Chippenham, Wiltshire

Contents

Acknowledgements

The authors would like to express their sincere thanks to all those who have made a contribution in any way to the writing of this book. In particular, Mr Christopher Satterthwaite Chief Executive of Chime Communications plc, Mr James Barkhouse Head of Country UK and Ireland for Syngenta Crop Protection UK Ltd, Mr Andrew Cottrell Head of Marketing for Syngenta Crop Protection UK Ltd, Mr David Jackson Managing Director of Click Tools Ltd and Mr Simon Emery Managing Director of Crown Lift Trucks Ltd for giving of their precious time so generously and for being so honest and open with the information about their organizations. Thanks also go to Dr Jane Spiro for her generosity in allowing her story 'Eye and the Fellow Traveller' to be reproduced in the book.

Further acknowledgements must be made to Professor David Hargreaves, Associate Director Specialist Schools and Academies Trust (SSAT), Emeritus Fellow Wolfson College, Cambridge; Professor Brian Caldwell, Managing Director of Educational Transformations Pty Ltd, Associate Director iNET (SSAT); Professor Y C Cheng, Vice Principal, Hong Kong Institute of Education and Professor Keri Facer, Professor of Education, University of Manchester, formerly Research Director, Futurelab.

Foreword

Life in the twenty-first century is making increasing educational, social, commercial, political and psychological demands on all those who are in the system. It is no longer good enough to manage organizations in the way they were managed in the twentieth century. To do so would ensure processes stagnating at a point when society demands huge leaps forwards. It is the cry of business, commerce, science and employment generally that the schools of today are not providing trained young people who have the work skills required by different facets of society. If this is true, then it is imperative that the issue is addressed as a matter of urgency.

The nature of society is changing faster than at any time in history and there would seem to be a time lag in educational organizations catching up with the perceived and actual skills young people need to take a comfortable and productive place in the local and global society and the world of work. Schools are clearly one member of a group partnership with parents, employers, society and the students themselves all of whom are charged with making this change happen.

Using educational institutions as a template, the rationale for this book is twofold. First to act as a guide to show how organizations can approach this problem and to encourage others to be creative and imaginative in their approach to leadership, this in turn will help their students, workers or clients to achieve in a changing world. The secret is to be bold and adventurous in thinking and implementation. Secondly, it aims to provide a narrative in a universal language applicable to all types of organizations.

In the middle years of the last century, schools were managed by authoritarian heads with little sharing or collegiality with colleagues; this inevitably led to an autocracy of the decision making process. While this was seen to be acceptable in some schools which were content to provide multitudes for low paid, low intellectually demanding jobs at one end of the scale, it did not encourage the top 1per cent of intellectually able students to attain University status at the other end, there was little spark or enthusiasm for real educational development which would allow all students to access a wide range of skills.

Times have changed: schools, like many other organizations, are altering their leadership framework. St John's School, Marlborough, Tesco Ltd, Prêt a Manger and the Wetherspoon Group plc are examples of organizations from different places in society who have recognized a need for altering the traditional hierarchical management structure to a sleeker, flatter model to facilitate collegiality of response and quicker decision making. Leaders here are leading, not just managing.

Using the school model, two things needed to happen to accommodate a change in philosophy. The management structure needed to change to address the way schools were now required to operate, and the curriculum needed to change to allow students access to the skills that the workplace now required. For example, the curriculum was addressed at St John's School in a skills based curriculum based on the 1999 Royal Society of Arts (RSA) Opening Minds Project (Bosher & Hazlewood 2005). This change in pace and emphasis was recognized by a change in the way schools were managed and reacted to external pressures from Government and from the community that the school serves. Costen (2007) notes that:

> education is a service industry. In state schools, management at all levels is based on the Government being the customer. By contrast, private education sees its customers as its students and their parents, and it has in view the higher education establishments or future employment to which students aspire. State education management is based on an over-prescriptive, test oriented national curriculum with an associated testing structure designed to provide hard data to monitor government targets, and an inspection system which focuses on test data and targets analysed by a government minded private contractor. The top down management structure is incoherent.

While this is a polemic with an independent school bias, there is some basis for the criticism levelled. Not all state schools are so tightly bound to the government strictures and many recognize the customer base as its students and their parents. Without doubt, there is a case for state schools to shake off the shackles of over prescription and develop both leadership / management styles and curricula that suit the needs of the student body.

With the development of new technologies, employers have started to recognize that the end product of the educational process was no longer providing a workforce with the necessary skills for the work place.

This book will address the leadership challenge of creating an environment for the development needs of a twenty-first century student. These students need to be globally aware, flexible in approach and develop transferable multi-skills across a wide spectrum of employment opportunities. The students need to be numerate, have highly defined social and communication skills, a *commitment to the work ethic* (Simon Emery, Crown Lift Trucks) and an Information and Communication Technology skill base embedded within all that they do. Employers in industry and commerce would argue for the same attributes for its workforce.

In order to create the appropriate learning environment, every organization must address as a first priority the way it is led. Looking forwards, schools must use their crystal balls to second guess needs for the future and put robust structures in place to facilitate those needs.

This book will show how such a culture change is possible, note the barriers encountered and the successes achieved. The book will focus on the values of 'the professional', professional autonomy, intellectual networking and federations. There needs to be a distinct move from the military style of command and control of old towards a value driven collegiate model which, it will be argued, is the way for the future.

Introduction

Schools can be considered to be a major vehicle for cultural transmission. The specific role for any school is to transmit the accepted and determined wisdom, knowledge and culture from one generation to the next. There is some suggestion that those 'in the system', that is, children, are being prepared for the future but in such a way that the past is ever present. The prevailing political fixation with league tables, target setting both for schools and for the individuals within them, contextual added value and success criteria all create a climate in which schools are fearful of innovation (in case it goes wrong), are suspicious of 'freedoms' and feel driven relentlessly to achieve ever higher, ever better. Are these the conditions for learning and education in the twenty-first century that will bring about improvements, real improvements to education, or are they the result of accountability requirements?

The latter years of the century also found a common voice among employers in commerce and industry who believed that the product of the school system was not properly prepared to be an active and useful contributor. All too often the school leaver needed 're-educating' for the purposes of the work place.

The world of the twenty-first century is one that is both rapidly changing and increasingly uncertain. Four- and five-year-olds entering the educational system now will leave to take their place as adults in society in 2019 (age 18) or 2021 or 2024 (graduation). But is the system likely to provide the education that these young people will need or will it provide a version of the twentieth century and nineteenth century diet marginally modernized but fundamentally the same?

The response by Government has been to focus on the personalization of learning as an attempt to redress the balance between education and 'the world of work'. Through policy documents such as Every Child Matters (DfES 2004) and The Children Act (DfES 2004), the 'top down' approach to school reformation has continued apace. However, the real danger is that increasing the pressure on schools and school leavers will create a vortex of confusion and lack of clarity. While rigorous and time consuming (time diffusing testing remains in place) the freedom for schools to create a truly personalized curriculum aligned with the needs of the individual, of society, industry and the environment, will be consigned to failure. Personalization of learning, by definition, demands personalization of assessment and validation. The en mass approach to testing simply reinforces the requirement for schools to conform to a rigid structure. Therefore the 'big question' remains: how do schools prepare learners effectively to be full participants in the global community? How do schools manage this feat and is there a commonality or synthesis of practice that brings schools and business together to utilize the human potential to the fullest extent?

This book addresses these issues. In our earlier publication *Nurturing Independent Thinkers* we explored a radically different curriculum approach that placed learners at the centre of the curriculum, one that gave them the power to shape their own learning journey and the responsibility to become fully independent learners and thinkers. This approach has proved over time to be very successful – Ofsted's (Office for Standards in Education) view not just ours! – but one that has far reaching implications for curriculum, examination systems and school management. However, the messages contained in this book are not only applicable to schools and other educational organizations but the management of all organizations. If the world is truly a rapidly changing environment, which few would disagree with, then the ability of all organizations to respond quickly and coherently to change is vital. This implies that all employees within the organization are fully aligned with company policy and thinking, feel involved in the direction of the company and empowered to act in the interests of company success. This is a complex and potentially precarious set of parameters but ones which some of the world's most successful organizations have already adopted. However, it is also true that the system of education in England does not actively and purposefully support either the present or the future needs of such companies. The product of 11 years of compulsory education is all too often disabled as a free thinker because the system demands a rigorous box like curriculum that is assessed in an introspective and limited way. No wonder some universities are setting their own entrance examinations to select leavers who show aptitude for thinking beyond and outside 'the box'. But what of the countless thousands of others that the system is failing? Charles Handy (1984) argues that

> the secondary school is not organized around the pupil as a worker but around the pupil as product. Raw material is passed from work station to work station, there to be stamped

or worked on by a different specialist, graded at the end and sorted into appropriate categories for distribution. The secondary school is the definitive sorting mechanism and it leaves an indelible impression. That so many come through it, smiling, grateful and grown up, is a tribute to the dedication of many teachers who impose their humanity and personality on those huge processing plants.

Handy goes on to say, 'others . . . leave alienated by an institution that seems to them oppressive, irrelevant and dismissive of their possible contribution to the world.' Written in 1984, 25 years ago, for the vast majority little has changed.

The poem written by Nukerji (1980) gives a clear view of the educational experience and one, that if the world is to survive, must change. The change is needed now and managing the political, economic and organizational environment to bring about this transformation is essential.

About School
He always wanted to say things. But no-one understood.
He always wanted to explain things. But no-one cared.
So he drew.
Sometimes he would just draw and it wasn't anything. He wanted to carve it in stone or write it in the sky.
He would lie out on the grass and look up in the sky and it would be only him and the sky and the things inside that needed saying.
And it was after that, that he drew the picture. It was a beautiful picture. He kept it under the pillow and would let no-one see it.
And he would look at it every night and think about it. And when it was dark, and his eyes were closed, he could still see it.
And it was all of him. And he loved it.
When he started school he brought it with him. Not to show anyone, but just to have it with him like a friend.
It was funny about school.
He sat is a square, brown desk like all the other square, brown desks and he thought it should be red.
And his room was a square, brown room. Like all the other rooms.
And it was tight and close. And stiff.
He hated to hold the pencil and the chalk, with his arm stiff and his feet flat on the floor, with the teacher watching and watching.
And then he had to write numbers. And they weren't anything.
They were worse than the letters that could be something if you put them together.
And the numbers were tight and square and he hated the whole thing.
The teacher came and spoke to him. She told him to wear a tie like all the other boys. He said he didn't like them and she said it didn't matter.

After that they drew. And he drew all yellow and it was the way he felt about morning.
And it was beautiful.
The teacher came and smiled at him 'What's this?' she said. 'Why don't you draw some-
thing like Ken's drawing? Isn't that beautiful?'
It was all questions.
After that his mother bought him a tie and he always drew airplanes and rocket ships like
everyone else.
And he threw the old picture away.
And when he lay out alone looking at the sky, it was big and blue and all of everything,
but he wasn't anymore.
He was square inside and brown, and his hands were stiff, and he was like anyone else.
And the thing inside him that needed saying didn't need saying anymore.
It had stopped pushing. It was crushed. Stiff. Like everything else.

(Nukerji 2003)

St John's School and Community College is an 11–18 co-educational comprehensive school of 1500 students that 'threw out the National Curriculum' at Key Stage 3 in 2001. This radical step was a response to the fact that however hard the school worked, both staff and students, continued improvement was reaching a plateau. The need to rethink both the curriculum and how learning was constructed became a burning issue. It was clear that the National Curriculum got in the way of learning and that the future needs of the world of work and of the human race were not going to be met by a curriculum predicated in the 1960s however excitingly rebranded into a personalized curriculum that it became!

The following chapters discuss the evolution of the curriculum approach at St John's and the very significant implications for management structures in schools and, by extrapolation, all organizational structure.

Chapter 1 explores the revolution in curriculum design and the evolving nature of management and leadership in a transformational setting. The conflict between the teacher as professional and leadership in schools is explored in this scenario.

Chapter 2 addresses the issues of moving from a culture of dependence to independence focusing on the role of core values and beliefs in creating the forward strategic direction. The shift required in leadership to accommodate this cultural translocation and ensuring the compatibility of the culture with those engaged in it is considered. The emerging nature of professionalism is developed.

Chapter 3 uses St John's as a case study to show how organizations can manage a major internal change which is brought about by external influence. It unravels the change parameters and the various influences that affect the change process. It also tracks the evolution of the leadership concept as the change moves ahead.

Chapter 4 embraces the new paradigm of collegiality that emerges as 'the way forward'. It examines the power of the concept and argues its centrality in organizational evolution to meet the challenges ahead.

Chapter 5 begins to see the difficulties of bringing a revolution in leadership practice into being and the intricacies of leading change while appearing not to!

Chapter 6 delves further into the case study and the interrelationship between leadership, collegiality and curriculum innovation. It seeks to examine the barriers encountered and the strategies through which obstruction and negativity can be minimized and defeated.

Chapter 7 draws together the strands of the case study and focuses on the future and the relative unpreparedness of the world to deal with complex and uncertain futures. Collegiality in a global context defines a way forward for educational leadership and development that seeks to provide a model for releasing learners to fully participate in the educational. The journey becomes one of co-operative engagement, all learners of whatever age fully owning their own educational pathway. The concept of 'professional' is rewritten to emphasize the process of collegiality is about collective accountability and responsibility for those engaged in education, it places leadership in a different conceptual place where the future is predominant, not the present.

1 Innovation and radical thinking in practice

By definition innovation requires a starting place. Usually it emerges from a perceived need, as the response to frustration or because the time in question demands a radically new direction. In a sense the St John's curriculum was a response to all three. Following the introduction of the GCSE examinations (replacing CSEs and GCEs) in 1987 and the National Curriculum in 1988, the school curriculum in England became increasingly blinkered, inwardly focused on a prescriptive list of areas to be covered within each subject. At one level it all seemed eminently sensible – every child covering the same areas of experience and content within defined time frames and being tested for progress at regular intervals. However, as the 1990s marched onwards the realization of what a state imposed curriculum meant in reality began to dawn. It had created a world of target setting, comparing school with school and thereby teacher with teacher. The resulting fear and pressure experienced by the teaching profession to perform, ably assisted by periodic Ofsted inspections, killed real curriculum creativity stone dead. Stepping 'outside the box' was definitely a high risk strategy only contemplated by those with a professional death wish! Or at least that was the experience from within. To consider change or question the logicality of the curriculum laid down in statute was only done academically; change in practice was a step too far!

However, in the solidification phase of a National Curriculum the world continued to move rapidly onwards moving out of the twentieth century, which the National Curriculum had been designed in and primarily for, and headlong into a very uncertain new millennium. For some in education, increasingly frustrated by a process in which 'professionals' were dictated to, the time to remain passive had gone. It had become increasingly obvious that the sort of education being 'given' to our children was not preparing them for the world that they would be entering, and indeed were already in.

A child born in 2000 would enter the work place somewhere between 2016 and 2022; did anyone seriously believe that a curriculum predicated on one that existed in the 1960s and 1970s would be remotely adequate for 2022?

The beginnings of a 'revolution'

In 1998 the RSA had commissioned a paper on the World of Work in the twenty-first century (Bayliss 1998). This clearly set the picture of a world of rapidly changing contexts, problems and the need for a flexible, responsive workforce able to adapt, be resilient and to think for themselves. In other words a cultural shift was needed towards independent, resourceful workers able to adapt to perhaps many different jobs through their lifetimes. This led to a second publication which took the second question, 'if this is what the world of work will look like what will education need to look like to bring this about?' *Opening Minds; Education for the 21ˢᵗ Century* (*Redefining the Curriculum*, Bayliss et al. 1998) provided a challenge. The least of the challenge was to recognize that in a world rich in Information Communication Technology (ICT), instantaneous communication, rapidly expanding access to data and information, the 'old' curriculum was no longer fit for purpose. Similarly the strategies for learning needed a substantial rethink.

St John's School and Community College had long been regarded as a 'good school'. This was a view shared by all concerned – parents, students, neighbouring schools, Ofsted and the community at large. However as the school worked towards further improvement it became increasingly difficult to match change and improvement to effort. Indeed the law of diminishing returns described the school's overall performance. The teaching force was working exceptionally hard but results only improved by small increments. The potential limit, based on standard tests for pupil attainment, had been reached. However, all involved knew more was possible but not by flogging an already flagging horse! Much of this is documented elsewhere (Bosher & Hazlewood 2005; Hazlewood 2003, 2004); suffice to say that to achieve further improvement a radical step needed to be taken.

The radical step, the innovative step, became clear in early 2001. Imagine life for a child entering school in Year 7, the experience should display continuity with the previous six years; it should show progression and incremental deepening relevant and related to the particular experiences and abilities of the participants. And yet for many the experience fell short. Twenty-five one-hour lessons per week taught by up to 14 different teachers none of whom really seemed to know what anyone else was teaching! Maths teachers had a clear view of the Maths syllabus, but no idea about Science, English and so on and certainly no plans to co-ordinate areas of common experience or spot learning connections to exploit for deeper learning opportunities. In short the curriculum was compartmentalized, lacking in coherence, lacking in connectivity and probably worse, duplicating experiences in ignorance rather than in a planned way.

This is not a criticism of very hard working and talented professionals, who give heart and soul to their profession, but it is an indictment of a culture of national obedience to an archaic curriculum model and of one that defines by implication what is acceptable in management practice. The expectation that school managers, that is, Headteachers and others, will ensure the delivery of the National Curriculum, ensure that students are prepared for the national tests, will do better year on year, in comparison both with the school's previous performance and in comparison with similar schools nationally, as the key requirement of 'successful leadership', hints of a world in which militaristic obedience is paramount. It also hints at a world in which reality is becoming blurred with fantasy. Continual improvement (i.e. better results year on year especially compared with similar schools who are attempting the same feat!) is not actually achievable. Political idealism and the practice of education do not always lie easily side by side.

There has to come a point in which true leaders stand up for what they believe in, stand up for those whose futures have been entrusted to them and speak out where injustice is being done. Injustice in this case is a failure to educate appropriately and thereby deny the children of today the most effective educational preparation for tomorrow. Far more seriously the very future of society in a global sense is imperilled by shortsighted political dogma.

In 2001 this was the step that St John's took, to 'throw out the National Curriculum' and create a curriculum which prepared students for life in the twenty-first century. As one of a small number of pilot schools for the RSA's Opening Minds Curriculum St John's was the only one to take the step of abandoning the National Curriculum and, in its stead, create a curriculum founded on five 'core competencies', as listed in Figure 1.1.

> - Learning to learn
> - Managing information
> - Managing relationships/relating to people
> - Managing situations
> - Global citizenship

Figure 1.1 Core competencies

The RSA Opening Minds competences

Developing a competence-led curriculum

In *Opening Minds* five categories of competences are proposed. Each category contains a number of individual competences, which are expressed in terms of what a school student could achieve having progressed through the curriculum.

Competences for learning

Students would:

- understand how to learn, taking account of their preferred learning styles, and understand the need to, and how to, manage their own learning throughout life
- have learned, systematically, to think
- have explored and reached an understanding of their own creative talents, and how best to make use of them
- have learned to enjoy and love learning for its own sake and as part of understanding themselves
- have achieved high standards in literacy, numeracy and spatial understanding
- have achieved high standards of competence in handling information and communications technology and understand the underlying processes.

Competences for citizenship

Students would:

- have developed an understanding of ethics and values, how personal behaviour should be informed by these, and how to contribute to society
- understand how society, government and business work, and the importance of active citizenship

- understand cultural and community diversity, in both national and global contexts, and why these should be respected and valued
- understand the social implications of technology
- have developed an understanding of how to manage aspects of their own lives, and the techniques they might use to do so – including managing their financial affairs.

Competences for relating to people

Students would:

- understand how to relate to other people in varying contexts in which they might find themselves, including those where they manage, or are managed by, others; and how to get things done
- understand how to operate in teams, and their own capacities for filling different teams roles
- understand how to develop other people, whether as peer or teacher
- have developed a range of techniques for communicating by different means, and understand how and when to use them
- have developed competence in managing personal and emotional relationships
- understand, and be able to use, varying means of managing stress and conflict.

Competences for managing situations

Students would:

- understand the importance of managing their own time, and have developed preferred techniques for doing so
- understand what is meant by managing change, and have developed a range of techniques for use in varying situations
- understand the importance both of celebrating success and managing disappointment, and ways of handling these
- understand what is meant by being entrepreneurial and initiative-taking, and how to develop capacities for these
- understand how to manage risk and uncertainty, the wide range of contexts in which these will be encountered, and techniques for managing them.

Competences for managing information

Students would:

- have developed a range of techniques for accessing, evaluating and differentiating information and have learned how to analyse, synthesize and apply it
- understand the importance of reflecting and applying critical judgment, and have learned how to do so.

Every aspect of every day had these strands woven through the children's' experience. Subjects were abandoned in favour of an integrated curriculum experience in which modules of six weeks duration became the vehicle for the development of the curriculum experience. An example of this is as follows:

Making the news module – there are no limits
An overview of a 'science' input across a full module

The rich possibilities within an integrated approach to curriculum delivery can be truly exciting for the teacher as well as for the student. The following outline provides a view of the areas covered by the students over the six-week module, 'Making the News'. This represents the input of one teacher for four, one-hour periods over the six weeks but it is interconnected with the work of other colleagues teaching the same group. Science, mathematics, technology, philosophy, critical thinking, history, astronomy and English are all encountered albeit with the same teacher.

The module begins with the question, 'What is the news?' The usual array of answers leads to the statement, 'What is news to you may not be news to me; discuss'. This begins to encourage the students to realize that a simple idea that we all take for granted can be much more complex. The idea that news can be both immediate and infinite raises many more questions. For example, our relative lack of awareness as time moves on is illustrated by the question, 'What was happening on other parts of the planet when Jesus was born?' The idea that human history focuses on key events and ignores or minimizes other 'news' is an important one but it also allows the development of critical questioning. Creating independent thinkers has, to an extent, been marginalized in the curriculum at Key Stage 3 and beyond.

In this module the ability to engage in debate is strongly developed through a process of raising questions that challenge the students' knowledge and understanding. Increasingly the teacher merges into the background accepting that he doesn't know all of the answers – far from it! The setting of the scene in this module is very much that it is a learning journey for everyone, teacher as well as student. While there are lesson plans the students know that they are negotiable. If an alternative line of enquiry emerges then the planned lesson goes and the class plan the replacement lesson. 'Homework' isn't actually set by the teacher; the group decides what is needed for the next lesson. For the continuation of their studies *at home* they will try to find the answers to the questions that they themselves have posed.

The sequence of the next few lessons begins to unravel some of the mysteries uncovered by the concept of 'news'. Timelines are used to create a picture of news at important moments over the last 3,000 years, and the ways in which humans communicated this news are explored. Some of the work would be familiar to any Year 7 student (the ear, the eye, messages in pictures, written communication, TV, radio, mobile phones) but the

Integrated Curriculum approach does not recognize limits. Therefore to understand the science of communication these students study the particulate nature of matter, calculate the speed of sound, discover how sound waves travel, investigate reflection, refraction, echoes, sound absorbency of materials and discuss emotional intelligence and 'sixth sense'. Angles, and calculations involving angles, are part of the 'discovery' but sine of the angle also comes in to help calculate refractive index.

In other parts of the story another teacher is looking at other aspects of news in the Norman Conquest. This provides an opportunity to look at some inventions in the past; in this case the trebuchet as a weapon designed to throw large objects at castle walls seems an obvious candidate.

The best way to understand, based on the research from previous lessons, is to build your own. The students embark on a design programme: first of all teams of designers and engineers are created; each person has a specific role depending on their strengths agreed by the group. The design is planned on paper, materials are ordered, measured, cut to size, structural matters such as angle of uprights to the base (for maximum strength) and methods of construction are agreed and the team go to the workshop to build the trebuchet.

Each team, after a period of trialling and modification, enters the self-directed competition to find out whose trebuchet is most effective. Finding out which one throws the projectile furthest is probably obvious, but the quality of the thinking that led to these designs demands a far more rigorous analysis of design strength and weakness. The competition included best design, best craftsmanship, strongest structure (measured by the load that the machine could support) and most original. It was the distance of 'projectile flight' aspect that was so surprising. The students realized that the flight of the projectile was actually an arc not a straight line and proceeded to try to calculate the distance travelled by the projectile. The final step resulted in the use of tangents drawn on the curve of trajectory. All of this was completely unaided: initially one group 'discovered' the idea and quickly shared it with the others. The significance of this finding for a class of 11-year-olds is quite remarkable given that even able mathematicians are unlikely to try this work before the age of 15 or 16.

The story of the trebuchet did not stop here. The group decided that they needed to do more work on forces and motion to get a better understanding of their inventions. Force = mass × acceleration, force due to gravity and velocity/time graphs all came into *their* lesson plan. (Hazlewood 2005)

Small teams (6 or 7) of teachers planned each module together and taught/facilitated learning across subject boundaries. The entire experience of the child was seamless, coherent, integrated and challenging. The philosophy was simple and yet demanding: 'to create learners who love learning so much that they can learn whatever they need whenever they need to do so' (Holt 1965).

If learners in the twenty-first century were to be resilient, resourceful and equipped with a portfolio of skills that helped them overcome any barriers, they would, above all, need to be confident and to accept full responsibility for their own learning. The step into the twenty-first century curriculum would necessarily have to be a step into independence of thought and action and away from the restrictive manacles of twentieth century National Curriculum structure.

The detail of this curriculum and its very considerable positive impact on learners and the national psyche is documented in *Nurturing Independent Thinkers*. However, its living legacy was to provide a real and difficult challenge to the management of the school as an organization at all levels. Empowering learners is one thing, giving them real power is quite another. Altering the working frame of reference for teachers and support staff placing the learner in a position to decide the direction of the lesson, take tangential learning routes also raises the challenge of the autonomous professional within an organizational context of mutual accountability, by action and outcome.

In the creation of a curriculum developed and owned by small cross-disciplinary teams of teachers the lines of accountability were also changed. The individuals in the teams were accountable to each other and to the curriculum school for the quality of teaching and learning. This proved to have a far higher threshold of direct accountability in that each teacher was at the 'sharp end' – there was no hiding place – every lesson mattered, it formed part of a whole in which the next phase of each journey would be continued with another member of the team. It raised the question of the role of Heads of Department. No longer was curriculum control within their remit; it lay with the teacher and the team and the children. Self-directing learners with teachers increasingly facilitating learning rather than leading learning, moves the locus of decision making.

Management models, schools and commercial organizations

Schools for many years have adhered to hierarchical models of management. Schein (1984) categorized such organizations as those in which:

- truth comes from those with positional power
- people need to be directed in the carrying out of instructions and supervised to ensure that it happens

1. TQM leadership is about imagination, enabling and empowerment of the rank and file – not about status;
2. The role of the TQM leader is to activate, coach, guide, mentor, educate, assist and support his or her colleagues so that they focus on a shared vision, strategy and set of intended outcomes;
3. TQM visionary leaders realize that it is cost effective to empower those nearest to a process to manage that process themselves;
4. TQM leaders concentrate on the whole picture and to keep it at the forefront of peoples' thinking;
5. TQM leaders also search for the small things that can make a critical difference;
6. TQM leaders believe that challenge and fun go together – laughter is healing. (pp. 68–69).

Figure 1.2 TQM model

- relationships are linear and vertical
- each person has a clearly defined niche in the organization and
- the organization is responsible for taking care of its members

Despite some very influential work in terms of Total Quality Management (TQM) and schools in the 1990s (Murgatroyd & Morgan 1993) many schools today continue to have management structures that adhere to that identified by Schein. Murgatroyd and Morgan's TQM model, as detailed in Figure 1.2, was predicated upon certain characteristics of TQM leaders.

The tension between the two descriptors of leadership became sharply defined in the transformation of the curriculum. A high degree of risk taking, thinking laterally, sharing curriculum planning with children became a fundamental operating procedure and yet even the language of total quality management didn't quite describe the activity.

Hargreaves' (2006) description of the 21st Century Imaginary is a helpful conceptualization of the quantum leap that schools need to make in order to bring about a truly personalized curriculum but more importantly, an effectively managed curriculum (see Figure 1.3).

Hargreaves' description of the twenty-first century school providing personalized learning for all, recognizing that all learners are individuals with the right to determine

THE CONCEPTUAL FRAME FOR LEARNING CENTRED LEADERSHIP	
19th Century Educational Imaginary	*21st Century Education Imaginary*
Students are prepared for a fixed situation in life	Students' identities and destinations are fluid
Intelligence is fixed	Intelligence is multi-dimensional
Schools are culturally homogenous	Schools are heterogeneous
Schools of a type are interchangeable	Schools of a type are diverse
Schooling is limited for the majority	Schooling provides personalized learning for all
Schools have rigid and clear boundaries	Education is life-long for every student
Schools work on the factory model	Education is unconstrained by time and place
Roles are sharply defined and segregated	Roles are blurred and overlapping
Schools and teachers work autonomously	Schools and educators work in complex networks
Education is producer led	Education is user led

Figure 1.3 Conceptual frame for learning centred leadership (Hargreaves D. 2006; p. 45)

their own learning pathways is a far cry from the National Curriculum. The perceptive elucidation of schools as diverse, heterogeneous and involved in complex networks was welcomed by many. The big question (education always has big questions!) is how does this paradigm shift happen? This is, in essence, the purpose of this book, to provide an answer to that daunting question.

Drawing together the language of TQM and the reconceptualization of learning centred leadership, St John's began the second revolution – that of creating a twenty-first century school management structure. In the early stages of debating curriculum change it was clear that in order to bring about lasting change, the ground needed to be prepared to change perceptions of curriculum managers. The first step was to shift the 'departmental' subject concept to one of subjects working together in groups of subjects (e.g. Maths, Science, Earth Sciences). This was achieved by introducing four curriculum schools. The second step was to change the title of Head of Department to Director. The concept of 'Director' was someone who had vertical responsibility for the quality of teaching and learning in that subject, progression of students but also a responsibility for sharing, with the other Directors, an overview of the full curriculum. Almost inevitably the latter took second place to the former and subject Directors tended to re-engage with the introverted curriculum, looking inwards into a world that they both under-stood and felt comfortable with. The Alternative Curriculum approach of Opening Minds however challenged that almost 'safe' world. The options were to accept and embrace the risk or ignore this radical new approach and hope it would go away. How-ever, the Alternative Curriculum was proving to be a big success. The children thrived, the staff really enjoyed the freedom to teach beyond the box; visiting schools, of which there were many, were captivated by the 'new approach' and Ofsted (2007) considered that it was 'an outstanding example of curriculum innovation . . .'

Sustaining innovation is a huge challenge. Great ideas can very quickly wither on the vine if steps are not taken to create a framework upon which to build. Enthusiasts, almost by their nature, move on to other or higher things. If the infrastructure is not in place to replicate, model and develop the original innovation it simply disappears, engulfed by those who were fearful of the change or otherwise opposed to it. The status quo of the tried, tested and familiar is a place where many retire to gratefully after the exposure and uncertainty brought by innovation and innovators!

In the development of the St John's curriculum 20 teachers were involved in the initial module creation, forming three teams of six or seven who taught the original three pilot groups. In the second year this rose to 70 teachers as the project rolled out to the full year group. The leadership of teams very quickly fell out of the Directorate structure largely because integrated teams did not have a subject leader but also because enthusiasts relished the opportunity to forge ahead with their developing teams and ideas generation. These enthusiasts were both established teachers and those new to the profession. Inadvertently the 'old' 'time on the job' concept which dictated that only those with a certain amount of experience could be leaders was evaporating. Credibility became directly related to team success and quality of ideas. Integrated team members progressed more rapidly in professional terms in two years than many who had been in post for 20+ years in more traditional structures.

A vital part of this evolutionary trend was not to fall into the trap that the manage-ment structure is set in stone but to release colleagues to find new approaches. The ethos quickly became one of a professional body trusted to take risks. The message was con-sistent – 'if you have good ideas, try them out – don't be afraid to take risks – if they work, great we move on, if they don't then a lesson has been learnt!'

As the Opening Minds Curriculum grew in success for the children and their teachers, it was also gaining a national and international reputation as one way to create a curriculum appropriate for twenty-first century learners. It became increasingly clear even the modified management structure was declining in relevance and was actually blocking further development. The scenario had become one in which Years 7 and 8 (11/12 year olds) were encouraged to be independent learners who then moved into the old subject orientation of GCSEs and the consequent culture of depersonalisation and 'success' by outcome. As a response to the post-16 needs of students who had grown through the Alternative Curriculum the International Baccalaureate (IB) was introduced in addition to AS/A2 levels. The IB, with its requirements that every student followed a broad range of subjects including English, Maths and a language supported by Theory of Knowledge and the Creativity, Action and Service programme, was far more aligned with the integrated, holistic experience of Years 7 and 8.

However, the problem of competing cultures remained. On the one hand a vibrant curriculum focused on learners, empowerment, a world without boundaries, a high level of personalization and expectation through Years 7 and 8 and potentially post-16 was interrupted, on the other hand by the traditional GCSE dominated exam/course route. This became a source, for some, of confusion and for others an argument to resist change, after all the law dictates what schools must do!

Creating a new management structure

In a radical attempt to redefine the management of the curriculum, and avoid retrogressive cultural behaviours re-emerging, a new management structure was put into place. It was heavily underpinned by philosophy and a clearly defined ethos. The fundamental areas of management philosophy surrounded the concepts of 'professional' and 'professionalism'.

As long ago as 1975 Stenhouse distinguished between the restricted professional and the extended professional, as described in Figure 1.4.

Autonomous professional self development relies not only on reflection on personal performance but also on a high degree of interaction between self and others within

Restricted Professional
- a high degree of classroom competence
- child-centredness
- a high degree of skill in understanding and handling children
- derives high satisfaction from personal relationships with pupils
- evaluates performance in terms of his/her own perceptions of changes in pupil behaviour and achievement
- attends short courses of a practical nature

But the Extended Professional concept went further. It included the above but also the following:

- has a capacity to view work in the wider context of school, community and society
- participates in a wide range of professional activities
- is concerned to link theory and practice
- is committed to some form of curricula theory and mode of evaluation

Figure 1.4 Professional characteristics (Stenhouse 1975)

the profession. A fundamental part of the philosophy denies political interference in that the 'professional' is normally expected to have some degree of control over definition, delivery and maintenance of standards.

Managing and management in this context therefore goes beyond the distributed leadership model (Ritchie & Deakin Crick 2007) and seeks to focus all management activity around the process and practice of learning.

The heart of the ethos was that the school only exists for the education of the child – it has no other core purpose. For the child, every day matters and therefore the curriculum and all other experiences must be of high quality and place the learner at the centre of all endeavours. The vision for the school was simply 'a school where every individual matters and where people are valued for who they are and what they may become'.

Therefore in the creation of the management structure it seemed apposite to place the learner at the centre. Each management position should support the learner and the school's vision and not simply replicate archaic hierarchical structures based on a model more akin to a military organisation! In this type of structure the Head of Department, subservient to the Headteacher, Deputy Head and so on, with his/her second in command (the second in command department) has a key purpose – to 'deliver' the curriculum ensuring that both staff and students discharge their respective responsibilities to the best of their ability. And yet there seems to be a lack of logic operating; do professionals need to be told what to do, checked upon to ensure they've done it and have freedoms restricted by policy, departmental or otherwise?

There is clearly a need for agreed operating procedures and a common understudies of, and alignment with, the ambitious and strategic direction of the school, but beyond that the extended professional should be permitted the freedom to engage in 'Great Teaching'.

To establish a structure not bound by tradition of pattern and rituals, looking forwards to supporting learners to meet their needs and fulfil their potential, Directors were abandoned along with the second in command! In their place, building on the strength of integrated subjects, came four curriculum schools

- The School of Human Exploration (Maths, Sciences, Earth Sciences, Psychology)
- The School of Human Performance (Physical Education, Philosophy and Ethics, History, Sociology, Media, Arts, Music, Drama)
- The School of Human Communication (English and Languages) and
- The School of Human Enterprise (Technology, ICT, Business Studies, Economics)

The Curriculum School names were deliberately chosen to focus on the curriculum as principally the study of Human activity, impact and potential. Within each Curriculum School (each consisting of approximately 25–30 teaching staff with administrative support) Phase Progression Leaders for age 5–13 (primary–early secondary years) and 13–19 (middle secondary to the interface with higher education) were responsible for the progression of the individual child within subjects, the Curriculum School and *across* the school. Supporting their work Whole School Strategy Managers responsible for staff logistics, post-16 education, vocational and Diploma programme development, IB

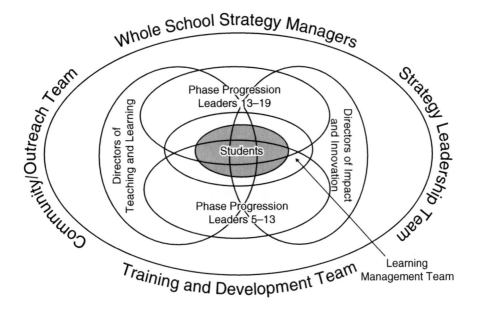

Figure 1.5 The collegiate staffing structure 2005

development, specialist college activity and data, analysis and examinations, created a whole school perspective (see Figure 1.5).

The curriculum schools were also partly a 'Trojan horse'. They acted as a focal point for dialogue around change while leaving a sense of the known and understood. The danger was that this might allow retrospective thinking and practice to continue. However, planned radical change must aim to take all of the participants with it, if at all possible. The alternative solution is to start afresh which, in organizational terms, involves a complex legal minefield and a disenchanted workforce. Research considers that fundamental change in the private commercial sector derive from the environment and international competition, while in education moral passion plays an important role. In terms of leadership in education a new paradigm is required which according to Marsh (1997) 'involves building a fundamentally fresh understanding of student learning . . . and developing a powerful new way of seeing how schools might be organised and conducted'.

The reality of cultural change is that one has to re-learn ones role and its inter-relationship with that of others. This proved to be a challenge of very considerable proportions. Despite almost a year of consultation and discussion with all parties prior to the change, with few if any objections, the new structure caused profound uncertainty. Despite a number of years of experience working as cross curricula teams in the creation and teaching of the Alternative Curriculum, working across the school as Phase Progression Leaders caused significant angst! However, the same was true for the wider role of Whole School Strategy Managers who now had a wide-ranging brief to bring about change wherever they saw direct benefit to the children and the school as a whole.

The driving force behind elimination of the traditional hierarchical structure of management to a truly flattened out one in which the student (client) was placed at the centre, was to establish the learner and learning as the central conversation. In reality the new structure was redefining professionalism in practice. In other words, leadership from all professionals would seek to 'create learning environments where all teachers are collaboratively engaged in deep learning' (McIver 2006). In the case of the Tasmanian model described by McIver this would be the task of the Principal. The St John's approach differed in that it expected all teachers to create this environment.

Caldwell and Spinks (1998) identified ten strategic intentions for a new professionalism:

1. Planned and purposeful efforts to reach higher levels of professionalism in data-driven, outcomes-oriented, team-based approaches to raising levels of achievement for all students;
2. Substantial blocks of time scheduled for teams of teachers and other professionals to reflect on data, devise and adapt approaches to learning and teaching, and set standards and targets that are relevant to their students;
3. Teachers and other professionals read widely and continuously in local, national, and international literature in their fields, consistent with expectations and norms for medical practitioners;
4. Teachers and other professionals become skilful in the use of a range of information and communications technology, employing it to support learning and teaching, and to gain access to current information that will inform their professional practice;
5. Schools (create) networks of schools and other providers of professional services in the public and private sectors to ensure that the needs of all students will be diagnosed and met, especially among the disabled and disadvantaged, employing the techniques of case management to ensure success for every individual in need;

6. Professionals work within curriculum and standards frameworks, as well as other protocols and standards of professional practice, with the same level of commitment and rigour as is expected in medicine;
7. Staff seek recognition of their work that meets or exceeds standards of professional practice and will support and participate in the programmes of professional bodies established for this purpose;
8. Schools ensure a much broader agenda than is evident in much of public discourse, including literacy and numeracy, and shall, without sacrificing attention to these, build their capacity to address a range of 'intelligences'.
9. The notions of 'the learning organization' and 'the intelligent school' will be embraced, and strategies will be designed and implemented to ensure success.
10. Schools will work with universities and other providers in a range of programmes in teaching and research and development that support and reflect the new professionalism in education.

Not all professionals understood what working with the same commitment and rigour as medicine meant, let alone what was meant by an 'intelligent school'. Consequently the starting points surrounded those aspects which were understood. Developing high quality data, team based approaches, setting achievable individual targets for every student gave a sense of common purpose and curiously a sense of 'getting there' with the new model.

From the perspective of the Phase Progression Leader (PPL) or strategy Manager (SM) this set of intentions seemed to be a work load that couldn't be surmounted. One of the difficulties was providing the time for people to meet (Strategic Intention 2) but it also emerged that a large difference existed between 'professionals'. At one end of a spectrum few read widely or exhibited rigour in standards of professional practice; at the other end exemplary professionals existed for whom this new management model was 'exciting, revolutionary and a challenge to be grasped' (Bosher 2008).

Describing and exemplifying the processes that each role had as common elements became a really important starting point. Helping colleagues to understand how their role worked, how it connected with the role of others and how to work across the curriculum rather than in vertical strands began to break the cycle of confusion. However, it took months to make the sort of steps that, at the beginning, had seemed so straightforward. The diagram (Figure 1.5) helped to locate the child at the centre of endeavour. It finally transcended the management models that invariably emerge, irrespective of structure, as hierarchical.

Frequent and precise talk about managing specific situations increased the momentum towards the new management practice and the understanding of the underlying philosophy. Full evaluations of the process of change were undertaken at given intervals (Wyse 2006; Bosher 2008) to plot the progress towards implementation but, probably as importantly, to reflect the concerns and aspirations of those within the structure.

Probably the largest single dilemma was the concept of 'freedom'. Given the freedom to take risks, to innovate, to make decisions without reference to a hierarchical framework and therefore seeking permission, was alien to almost all. This is perhaps not surprising; few, if any, had worked in an environment that did not emphasize accountability and subservience to a higher 'officer'. Rather, like a freed long term prisoner, accommodation to another world was difficult, a little frightening and mostly disconcerting.

The ultimate decision making entity was 'the team'. The team was described as that group of colleagues working together for common purpose. It could be to teach Maths, to examine an individual student's learning experience, to plan a sequence of integrated Year 7 lessons or to develop any aspect of the curriculum or related activity. Far from becoming the uncontrolled hydra that one could imagine, team decision making became a very careful matter. Clarity of thought, testing of ideas, common consensus became hallmarks leading to any decision. In part this was to avoid 'getting it wrong', in part it established a new working relationship and finally it really focused the conversation on benefits to the learner. No longer was a top down decision the defining rationale but a team grown solution to a commonly defined problem or situation.

Through the team evolution other issues began to emerge quietly at first and then rapidly increasing in voice. Non-teaching staff who previously had a supportive role almost doing the bidding of the Head of Department, now found themselves in a position of being a vital team member. Once the team had *decided* the task invariably fell to the administrator to organize. In one sense this was exactly what the model had envisaged and was implied by D. Hargreaves's (2006) conceptual framework for Learning Centred leadership. The blurring of roles created tensions between professional and non-professional. In a management model that emphasized the equality of people working together for common purpose (collegiality) inequality of status and pay became markers for discontent.

The concept of collegiality as a management model for twenty-first century organizations, irrespective of business focus, will be discussed in Chapter 4. Suffice to say 'take home pay' is a really hard divide to overcome with philosophy! However, this in a real sense is the new twenty-first century leadership paradigm and paradox. The paradox is neatly summed up in the Chinese proverb that *when truly great leaders have done their work the people say 'we did it ourselves'*. The paradigm revolves around redesigning management functions to allow high performing work teams' access to the information required to be fully informed and empowered. It is only a part of the paradigm. Change must be aligned with student success and therefore the function of the high performing work team must keep this in full view. This is the key to breaking the divide. Identification of the depth and breadth of professional expertise, direct contact with the learner in the process of development on the part of the professional and the skills and abilities of the administrator to bring about increased team effectiveness and efficiency, bridge the professional/non-professional divide. The knowledge that both need each other to succeed is powerful. Human nature however sometimes lags a little behind!

In the following chapters the continuing evolution of leadership will be explored from both an educational and commercial perspective. It is important to emphasize though that leadership and leadership styles are not fixed nor absolute. They need to respond to the needs of the organization both now and in the future. The future is the compelling question. How will organizations need to be led, managed, structured in 2025–2030? If learning, education and the workplace are to continue to evolve at such a fast rate, and they must if the planet is to survive, how will integrated thinking and management practice maximize the endeavour of the individual citizen?

2 Bringing about a change from dependency to independency

This chapter is not a commentary on the academic process of change *per se;* there are volumes of research aimed specifically at that area. The process of change must be addressed however in the way that it impacts on organizations and the leadership of them.

In any organization there comes a time when what is currently in place in terms of organizational processes, personnel or strategic direction is no longer fulfilling the purpose for which it is intended. When this becomes evident, the organization has two options. To stick its head into the sand and do nothing, leading to decreasing levels of effectiveness and performance but keep life happy and comfortable for those involved. Alternatively, the organization must 'grasp the nettle' and bring about change (whatever that means internally) in order to move forwards and continue to compete with similar organizations. Hopkins, Ainscow and West (1994: p. 21) recognize that there are two forms of change, the *incremental change* which takes place gradually over time and secondly *planned change* which can take place quickly. Incremental change can take place in a subtle manner gently moving from one position to another. Planned change on the other hand can be much more aggressive perhaps taking place at a single moment in time and breaking up completely what went before in order to bring about a new way of 'doing'. It must also be recognized that the impetus or pressure for change can originate from two sources. The first of these is internal pressure. This can develop over time as the organization follows trends or market forces, and the members of the organization recognize that different approaches are needed. Alternatively, the pressure for change can come from external forces. In the case of education, pressure can be exerted by the Local Authority, the Government, parents or the community. For commerce and business it will certainly be from market forces with whom the organization is competing.

From an educational perspective, the thrust for the 'brave new world' of the twenty-first century is to encourage all in the system to address societal change and to become more self sufficient and less dependent. For 150 years, education has led its students from point A to point B by telling them in a didactic manner. In an era of social control in the early twentieth century, the leaders of society did not want many who could or would think for themselves. The exclusive 'club of leadership' was jealously guarded with access only possible through jumping high hurdles that few were equipped to jump. A solid workforce of machine minders and manual workers who completed repetitive but low skilled tasks was what society required. Then the technological revolution happened.

The blaze of technology including computer driven machines, word processors instead of typewriters, electronic storage instead of paper files, computers to undertake mathematical calculations hitherto undertaken by slide rules and the like all brought redundancy to existing educational processes and practices. A 'new dawn' occurred when it became obvious to educators and participants alike that change had to occur to cope with this technological revolution. It was no longer good enough to expect workers 'just to do', there had to be an understanding of underpinning principles as well. This brought about the need for change from 'dependency to independency'. The existing dependency state of education had to move with the times. It does have to be recognized however that coming with this technological revolution and advanced thinking came an increase in a support capacity. Each advance brought with it a need to maintain the machines, provide IT support for the newly understanding operators and a change in processes and protocols for the integration of this technology into existing practice. In a strange way and at one level counter argument way, it added dependency to the system, not removed it. Without support, much technology malfunctions very quickly. Overall there was a move from dependency but brought recognition of an increased 'service' industry and a training need for supporting personnel.

As the twentieth century drew to a close, the educational establishment began to recognize that a fact based curriculum and teaching methodology had to be replaced. The RSA initiated its 'Opening Minds Project' in 1999 was an example of this. This was a planned change to an external influence that occurred in a very short period of time.

Vision, mission or intended direction by any other name?

In order for an institution to address changing needs for the future, it must start by examining its existing processes and leadership structures. Is change necessary, and what are the reasons for any proposed changes? Will they make the organization more efficient, more competitive, produce better results, and enable the institution to maintain or gain an improved position in the market place? The institution must ask itself if its existing structures are sufficiently flexible, dynamic and robust enough to carry change and innovation forwards in response to the demands of a changing environment. St John's School did just that in 2004. The Senior Management Team was renamed the Strategic Leadership Team as the first action. The new name carried with it a direct message about the type of approach which the leadership of the school intended to adopt. It is a way of getting into a new culture and the new terminology can open up new thinking skills and approaches that have been closed by many years of repressive terminology. This was an important message for all members of the community about leadership in the school. The Strategic Leadership Team sat down and did an in-depth analysis of how the school was led at the strategic level, and how it was managed at the middle levels. For the sake of reader clarity, this is the level of the Head of Department at curricular and academic levels, and Head of Year for those involved in pastoral issues of social care for students. In Chapters 1 and 4 the differences between leadership and management are explored in some detail, and it is quite evident that the day of the 'classic manager' is numbered. That is not to say that in any organization there are not management type activities to be undertaken. Quite the opposite, there will always be day to day activities that have to be performed in order to keep the wheels of the organization turning. However, there is the question of who is the most appropriate person or team of people to undertake these management type activities.

For the new world of the twenty-first century, the organization has to be brave and acknowledge that the time for radical thinking and of thinking beyond current boundaries has arrived. It is difficult to understand how on limited budgets with multiple demands on finite financial resources, organizations continue to pay very experienced and academically qualified staff to manage and administer activities like issuing text books, ordering resources or a multitude of other managerial tasks that could be performed by other members of the school or organizational team. Members of the support staff teams are just as well qualified to do those tasks, but do not possess teaching qualifications, the breadth of view or experience necessary to take the subject, department or area into the future. These activities can then be left to the teachers with those skills and experience.

Every school, institution or organization is different. The 'feel', 'tone', 'atmosphere' and general ambiance of each community will be unique. It is developed from the people who inhabit that particular world. In the case of a school, the culture develops as a result of the Headteacher with his or her educational philosophy, his / her experiences and his / her visions. These are added to by the teachers with their different skills, qualifications and experiences, the students with their own views, the supporting staff, the parents and communities around the school. All these subgroups contribute to what may be termed the culture of the organization. In fact, the inclusion of many different client groups within the organization enables the development of numerous subcultures, and it is the sum totals of these numerous subcultures which finally form the culture for that organization. Hughes, Becker and Geer (1971: p. 51) show clearly how subcultures develop.

> [S]ub-cultures of which student cultures are one example, develop best where a number of people are faced with common problems and interact both intensively and extensively in the effort to find a solutions for them, where people who face the same contingencies and exigencies in every day life have an opportunity to deal with these communally.

The development of these subcultures should not be seen as a threat by the organization, but embraced by it on the grounds that the true cultural flavour of the organization is going to be the sum of the individual contributions.

The reader should remember that any organization will have subcultures, formed in the same way with the same tensions and pressures, and the same rules apply for the development of the overall culture of the organization, it is the 'sum of the parts'.

If this premise about the development of an individual culture is accepted, then getting the leadership in place to motivate, promote and stimulate the development of that culture is the first of many important steps that the institution must address.

Creating the vision

The first step in the process has to rest with the leader of the organization. It has to be the visionary ideal of the Headteacher, the owner, the Chairman or the Chief Executive of a company who has to be clear about the direction in which the organization under his or her care must go. This vision development may be undertaken by a small team working with the chief executive as in the case of Syngenta Crop Protection UK Ltd (Syngenta) the global crop protection company, the individual aspiration of the Chairman, like the case of Chime Communications plc (Chime), the owner and his family in the case of Crown Lift Trucks, the Managing Director in the case of Click Tools Ltd or a Headteacher as in the case of St John's School and Community College.

In the case of Syngenta, the formation of the company in 2000 was the result of the amalgamation of two other crop protection companies. The new Chief Executive Officer (CEO) took his senior leadership team off site for a period of 'blue skies thinking'. They were determined to create two things for their new company. The first was to establish the direction in which the company was to go forwards and secondly to establish clearly what the organization actually stood for; 'what was their reason for being'. This was crucial to the company as it needed a new identity as it emerged from the merging of the two existing companies. It is rare that an organization can start with a blank sheet of paper but it does happen, and it is up to the leaders of the organization to grasp the opportunity for radical thinking. At the end of a week of intense discussion, the team came up with their vision statement. The brief was that it had to be clear, concise and understood by all members of the company and by the market in which Syngenta operates commercially. James Barkhouse, Country Head of UK and Ireland for Syngenta recognized that a clear mission statement was crucial to the company, but acknowledged that in many companies, mission statements are often poorly known, misunderstood or misinterpreted by the workforce. Syngenta therefore spent a great deal of energy following the creation of the mission statement ensuring that the company's strategic direction was reinforced regularly and understood by all 20,000 members of the workforce globally from the Chief Executive Officer to the receptionist, a formidable task. Syngenta created the type of ideas diagram described in Figure 2.1 to explain the flow of information to and from all members of the workforce.

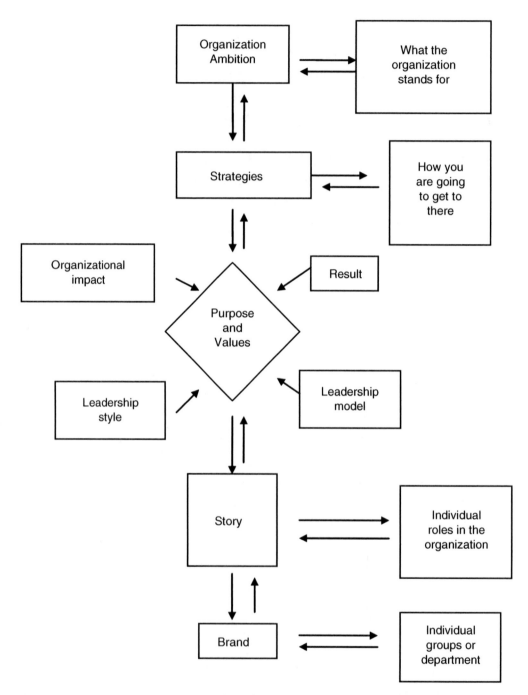

Figure 2.1 The Syngenta Crop Protection UK 'Backbone' model for disseminating values and beliefs through the system – a two-way process (based on the author's personal discussions with J. Barkhouse in 2008)

For Syngenta, this is a two-way process and the processes are similar for many different organizations. The terminology may differ according to the nature of the organization, but the two-way dialogue with feedback into the main system at several points is the key to creating a robust and flexible system which gives all members of the organization both access and ownership.

A different approach was employed by Chime Communications plc, an umbrella communications company. Under the leadership of its Chairman, Lord Bell, the organization is the parent company for 30 subsidiaries, and employs in the order of 6,000 staff. To create their mission statement, the Chairman together with Group Chief Executive Chris Satterthwaite had discussions with the Board of Directors to establish their core values and beliefs. Following agreement on these by the board, Satterthwaite was charged with formulating the mission statement. Once this had been produced, the Group Chief Executive realized that it was imperative that all 30 companies under the umbrella company also shared and agreed with the statement. To consolidate the work that he had done, Satterthwaite called all the senior 'thinkers' in the 30 companies together to launch the group mission statement, values and beliefs. A similar methodology might be undertaken by other organizations, with those in senior positions in the company deciding on direction, rationale and identity. Crown Lift Trucks Ltd were in a different position. They are a family-owned company employing 8,500 staff globally with 85 factories and offices spread across the continents. Because it is a family-owned organization, the three generations of the family who now control the company created their work ethic, values and direction within the family.

The route that St John's School took was a slightly different approach. Following a guidance paper from the Headteacher it was decided by the Strategic Management Team to harness the views of all the client groups associated with the organization. Several representative meeting were held, and each meeting was commissioned to develop statements about what the school stood for. This was done in a small table scenario with those trusty tools that all educationalists recognize, sticky notes and flip charts. The task was to gather words or statements which in the eyes of the community, groups and individuals captured the 'being' or the 'heart' of the school. What should the school aspire to now, and what will it look like in ten years time in the way it embraced its educational ideals, and is it an embedded part of the local community?

A cautionary note: If this type of collegial activity is undertaken, it is crucial that detailed and accurate briefings are held to ensure that the end product of the deliberations is in the form that is required. Experience showed that an imprecise set of briefing notes led to thought processes engaging in areas that were to produce inappropriate results later. This happened quite accidentally and was the result of different groups adding their personal perspectives, but not appreciating the main goal which was a mission statement which included and embraced the whole organization. What happened initially was that the thought processes were too narrowly focused, accentuating one perspective but missing the bigger picture of the organization in its entirety and without engaging the whole panoply of its activities, emphasis and directions.

After each meeting, the flip chart comments were collated, organized and ordered. An embracing series of statements was then produced which it was hoped reflected the feelings and ideals of each interest group. After all the meeting groups had met, the different strands of ideas were pooled. Inevitably, there was a degree of congruency among them all, but similarly there were also some profound differences. These differences arose out of the different perspectives, positions and standpoints that each of the client groups held.

Once the ordered statements were formulated, they were displayed and communicated to all participants for two reasons. One was to reassure the groups that all contributions were received and considered. This is an important public relations activity of transparency and one that leads to trust, openness and honesty. Secondly, it was important as a quality control mechanism to ensure that the appropriate emphasis and inflection had been captured in the production of the statements. It was for all client groups to verify this was the case.

These ideas were subsequently collated and prioritized by the Strategic Management Team. After discussion, a concise mission statement was produced. This again needed to be circulated to all client groups for final acceptance and understanding. Once this was agreed and passed by the Governing body, the *raison d'être* for the school could be published and publicized.

Outlined earlier are four ways in which the mission statement, values and beliefs of an organization can be formulated. They are different in approach, but exactly the same in outlook. They all shared the view that formulation is one thing, making it live and be part of the organizational life of the organization is another. To do that effectively, an agrochemical company, a communications company and a school all took immense trouble to ensure that the corporate message was disseminated throughout the organization, and continues to be so in the day to day life of the organizations.

Any organization then has the task of ensuring that all members 'live' that statement. To facilitate this, the organization must next turn its attention to the leadership / management structures at all levels. It is not sufficient for the senior members of the organization to sit smugly back with the knowledge that they know exactly where they are leading the company or school. Without the workforce and client group behind them, this strategy is doomed to failure. The old teaching adage *Fail to plan and plan to fail* is as true in areas of leadership as it is in teaching a lesson.

So how does an institution go about changing its leadership structure?

The organization has to be bold, confident and prepared to take risks. The lead has to come from the most senior person in the organization and Kark and Van Dijk (2007: p. 500) make the point that: 'Transformational and charismatic leadership is an influential mode of leadership that is associated with high levels of individual and organisational performance'. The leader must have these characteristics if the rest of the organization is to follow. Kark and Van Dijk (2007: p. 500) go on to confirm the important centrality of the main leader. 'Leadership effectiveness is critically contingent on, and often defined in terms of, leader's ability to motivate followers towards collective goals or a collective mission or vision'.

The leader plays a central and pivotal part in any visionary activity. This of course is not a new concept, but has been reinforced in conversations with organizations outside of education. What is equally important however is that the rest of the workforce and in the case of education the client groups also have a part in and share the message being promulgated. Andrew Cottrell, Head of Marketing from Syngenta UK makes the point that managers (the term used most commonly in business to denote those who have control of employees and often significant financial resources) must have 'clarity of objective duty to employees to articulate the company's stated beliefs and values'. Chris Satterthwaite, Group Chief Executive for Chime Communications plc holds a similar view that 'all employees are included in all that is done' and that in his company, he has recognized a truism that holds for all organizations when he says, 'Values stay the same, cultures develop and practice constantly changes'.

Chapters 1 and 4 discuss the various forms of leadership in some detail, and it is armed with the head leader's decision on the form of leadership to be employed that the discussions regarding the staffing structure can then be developed.

Using the case study example of St John's School, the commentary will now note the actions taken to establish a new staffing structure. The specific details of the structure will be addressed in Chapter 3, but the principles are noted here.

We will now look in more detail at the actions necessary to bring about change. Bear in mind that a management / leadership structure is already in place and functioning, and that in any organization there is an inbuilt reluctance or even resistance to change. It is necessary for the head leader to acknowledge this and to ensure that there is transparency and understanding in any proposed changes made to be made. Additionally, that true consultation, willingness to listen and to change and modify are part of the action plan.

At St John's the Strategic Leadership Team (SLT) led by the Headteacher met on numerous occasions to define and then implement an action plan. The nature of the meetings was in a conference framework with large portions of time allocated away from the day to day issues of managing the school to address the strategy to answer the questions in Figure 2.2. Adequate managerial cover had to be put into place to ensure the safe and efficient running of the school while these discussions were taking place.

The deliberations started with the structure of the Strategic Leadership Team itself. The Headteacher outlined his radical new thinking together with his rationale to support it. Many of the questions listed in Figure 2.2 were as pertinent to and affected the individuals in the SLT as they did to anyone else in the workforce. There were the personal dilemmas to be faced with some members apparently gaining status promotion while others felt that they had been passed over. Hard questions from the Bursar about the finances available within the school budget to make the necessary promotions at this level were also the focus of much discussion. This brings the conversation back

Why do we need to change the existing structure?
What will we achieve by changing the structure?
What is the time scale for implementing the new structure?
How will we know that the new structure will be better than / more effective than or more efficient than what exists already?
How will we monitor and evaluate the changes when they are made?
How will the workforce be informed of the new structure?
Will the workforce be given opportunities to discuss the proposals, make recommendations and make appeals?
Will the new structure disadvantage any member of the existing workforce?
Will there be a mechanism to accommodate and counsel individuals who have particular individual problems?
If so how will the organization compensate the person?
Can the organization financially afford any proposed changes?
Will the proposed changes offer new or extended career development opportunities for the workforce?
How will proposed changes affect the balance of decision taking and making in the organization?
Will there be a change in status for individual and will this unbalance the organization as a whole?
What will members of the workforce do who disagree with the restructuring decisions made?
Will there be an agreed senior leadership strategy in place to defuse discontent?
If staff chose to leave the organization, can the organization itself continue to work effectively in the interregnum before the appointment of new staff?
How will the changes be presented to the employers and in the case of the school, the Governing body?

Figure 2.2 Questions to ask

to the start of the chapter. Courageous, forward thinking individuals considered risk taking was required to bring about radical change. Fortunately the Headteacher of St John's was perceived by Ofsted 2005 to have these qualities in abundance and so progress was made. Once this structure was in place and agreed, the deliberations of the structure surrounding the SLT could then take place. All individuals in the team were dispatched with the task of developing models which satisfied the defined criteria and addressed the answers to the questions in Figure 2.2. Playing both 'devil's advocate' and the role of 'critical friend' members of the team achieved eventual agreement and congruency of thought.

Once the staffing structure was in place, specific scenarios were posed to test the model. The most difficult part of developing a new staffing structure centred on the detail of specific job roles. Unless these are clearly described, grey areas exist.

What is now being reviewed are the principals of how the leadership model is being changed. On one hand, the strategy of the Headteacher was to leave job specifications open ended. Collegiality was a new and developing concept in the school, and this approach requires open ended thinking. Collegiality as an approach will be discussed in detail in Chapter 4. On the other hand, from the majority of the workforce's point of view, unless closely described job specifications were available, they found it difficult to make sense of the structure and fully appreciate the new entity being created. This was a real dilemma for SLT to resolve. The move that St John's made in relation to collegiality was not isolated. For example, New Zealander David Barry (1991: Executive summary) referred to his concept of 'bossless teams'. Barry describes and applauds the concept of a 'distributed leadership system that works effectively with self managed teams'. Barry noted that many companies globally use variants on the idea. He notes that 'Digital, FMC, Frito-Lay, GE, General Foods, Hewlett Packard, Honeywell and Pepsi Cola, as well as many smaller firms', all use the concept. Barry (1991: p.1) does however articulate the central problem to be overcome if change of leadership strategy is to be achieved. That is; 'Most leadership theory adopts a person-centred approach, in which leadership is a quality that exists in one person – the leader.'

If you take the overt leadership influence away from the immediate environment, the group/s have to be secure in their understanding of any particular brief and be clear about the delegated decision making powers and responsibility that are now on the group's collective shoulders.

This then is the task which remains if the staffing structure is changed. Making it work is a corporate exercise which requires open-mindedness, a willingness to try new things, tenacity, patience and a degree of humility to accept and change when things go wrong.

Achieving the right culture and getting the culture right

Achieving the right culture is a difficult activity which requires patience, vision, confidence and time. Cultural changes do not and cannot take place overnight. To do new things which are different from what has been the status quo for the institution disturbs the existing balance. A consequence of change is that there are winners and inevitably losers in the process. This is also the case when bringing about a change in culture. As stated earlier in the chapter, culture develops from the sum of the subcultures which influence the institution. The task for the leaders of the organization is to decide what the new cultural direction is required, and when it is required by. This may sound a little strange to the reader, but it further emphasizes the need for the leader of the leaders to have a visionary outlook. The leader/s need to take a view of where the institution or organization is at the present time, consider what changes to a new cultural standpoint need to be made, what the new cultural position will be and the time by which the desired new cultural position needs to be in place.

These are all crucial decisions that need to be made prior to any changes being made. The workforce or group who are to be part of the cultural change will go through a series of emotions. Such feelings as fear, cynicism, apprehension, excitement and intolerance might be some of the emotions that will be experienced. Not by everyone, and not all at the same time, but they will be there. It has to be remembered that for some the change will be an uplifting experience opening doors to further career development opportunities. For others change may bring about or pose a threat. Many people are happy to sit in their 'comfort zone' be conscientious and do their job to the best of their ability but not wish to extend themselves. For people with this mindset change will inevitably be an uncomfortable experience. Others, maybe the cynics, will see any changes or proposed changes in a negative light. They may suggest that such changes are foolish, pointless, unnecessary or valueless to the organization. These are a particular group that need specific leadership focus.

Much research has been undertaken on school culture and the effects that culture has on innovation, and this book is not intending to follow that particular line in depth. Researchers such as Lawrence Stenhouse in the 1970s, Jean Rudduck, Jennifer Nias and Geoffrey Southworth in the 1980s and early 1990s have laid the foundations of a research data base on which cultural change can be measured. Hopkins et al. (1994) comment on the previous work of Fullan and Park (1981) in New Zealand noting that cultural change from the implementation of organizational or curriculum change in a school setting will involve the interaction of a number of different factors. Without doubt, culture can affect the structures in a school, but by the same token, structures can influence and develop specific cultures. Let us explain the tautology of this a little more. For some schools, the culture that exits in the surrounding community environment will have a pervasive effect in the school. If for instance the school is in a socially deprived area with little social aspiration in the community, then the attitude of the pupils will reflect these home influences. As a consequence, the school has to adapt its internal culture to one which is recognized and accepted by the pupils and the parents in order to maintain their support. Small successes may be all that the school can hope to achieve because of the power and influence of the community. In this way, the structure and management of the school is determined by the pervading culture. By the same argument, in some schools where a historical culture of success is a feature, then the structure of leadership, management and life in the school will reflect this. In this case, the structure will affect the culture of the school in perpetuating high performance and success. Fullan and Park (1981) note that it is the interaction of the key features in the organization that will bring about desired change. Changes to the structure in terms of its organization and policies, the use of new or different teaching materials, teachers acquiring new behaviours like changes in teaching styles and finally changes to some of the core beliefs and values that have hither to been associated with the school will all contribute to the change in culture.

With the benefit of this knowledge, St John's School embarked on a planned cultural change in 1997. This was a deliberate and intentional strategy on behalf of the then new Headteacher. The school in 1997 was a well established reasonably successful comprehensive school which was plateauing. It needed two things, a new direction and a new sense of purpose. The new Headteacher's arrival facilitated this.

The first and most important change was to cultivate the attitude of the teaching staff. He had in his mind the introduction of an alternative approach to learning using a skill based curriculum. To implement this sort of radical approach in the 1990s was going to need sensitive handling and a cool resolve. The existing culture in the school was examined and found to be effective but conservative in its educational approach. The school is a true comprehensive, located in the rural town of Marlborough in Wiltshire. As with many rural locations, the client group is composed of a majority of well-motivated, well-supported students from middle class environments. Additionally, the school population also contains students from more socially deprived rural backgrounds with supportive parents on lower financial budgets and as with all schools, a small majority of students and parents who place the value of education lower on their list of life's priorities. So getting the right culture and getting the culture right was the task in hand.

The chicken and egg conundrum was the task facing the Headteacher. The question was which to tackle first, the culture of the school or the right culture for his planned curriculum and teaching changes. He decided on getting the culture of the school in line with his thinking as his first priority. What the Headteacher envisioned was a teaching workforce that was prepared to understand and embrace educational change, see those changes for their educational merit, understand the underpinning educational philosophy and be prepared to experiment.

From a historical standpoint, teachers as a collective have always been conservative in their approach to their vocation, and have valued the autonomy which they enjoyed with their students when they closed the classroom door. To change that attitude while keeping the professional identity of each individual teacher intact was the mission.

From the whole school perspective the task was to ensure that changes to the structure in terms of its organization and policies were put into place so that the teaching staff felt support for what they were doing. The longer term direction of the school was clearly established and constantly reinforced. Job roles were reaffirmed and clarified. Timetables for both the teaching staff and the students were harmonized to make the teaching and learning process effective and streamlined, eradicating wasteful losses of time to ineffective processes. The timing of the school day was also addressed to accommodate the particular demands of the school (it is a split site school) which brings its own tensions and pressures. Monitoring, mentoring and quality control mechanisms were established to ensure that improvements were just that, improvements. External indicators and benchmarks like the Investors in People Award and the Charter Mark Award were sought and achieved to give the staff and the community confidence and credibility to the direction in which the school was going.

Teachers acquiring new behaviours like changes in teaching styles were always going to be a difficult obstacle to overcome. The insularity of the teachers in the classroom was required to change to a more 'open door' environment. Few teachers brought up in the middle years of the twentieth century were used to being observed. They considered such activity as threatening and that third parties in the classroom destroyed the individual chemistry between the teachers and their students. The change in 1992 to the new more open style of Teacher Education alleviated this feeling to an extent, and as those teachers developed into the middle management and became experienced practitioners, so the closed door apprehensions diminished. In the case of St John's there was a need for peer observation and team teaching to develop in preparation for the introduction of the 'Integrated Curriculum' initiative to be introduced three years later in 2001.

> **Authors' note:** This curriculum initiative changed its name as it developed. The initial name 'Integrated Curriculum' was changed to the 'Alternative Curriculum' after the initiative had run for 3 years (2003); this name was changed again at the request of Ofsted in 2005 to the Year 7/8 Curriculum.

Supporting these new teaching strategies there was a need for new or different teaching materials, particularly resources. To prepare the teaching staff for this substantial change, dedicated professional development opportunities were created. Specifically, there was a need to upgrade staff skills in the use of new Interactive White Boards, website use, computer aided design programmes, and computer aided machine use in technology, PowerPoint presentations, spread sheets and data bases. These technologies were then transferable into the classroom in the development of teaching resources, and also as tools for the students to use in their own right as they honed and developed their own skills.

Perhaps the biggest challenge of all was to make changes to some of the core beliefs and values. A new mission statement was created as described earlier in the chapter.

The school's mission statement

A school recognised for excellence in teaching and learning, that places the learner at the centre of all endeavour and that sets the standards to which others aspire. A school at the heart of its community, where everyone is valued for who they are, for what they may become and where people matter more than anything else. (Hazlewood 1997)

This new mission statement was a response to the recognition of the changing needs of its student population. It is a school which lives its mission statement and sees that statement as the guiding and directional force on which all activities including management are based. It is predicated upon the firm belief that the existing structure and content of schooling would not be appropriate for the educational needs of students in the twenty-first century.

The values and beliefs that radiated from this were far reaching, touched and involved all members of the school community. The major impact of this change in values is to make a strange admission. For the first time, the school made a public statement of the implied but obvious value that the 'child should be central to all that the school does and stands for'. Hitherto, such a basic value had been understood by most, but left unsaid. The consequence of which is that not all subscribed to the ideal but could not be criticized because it was not formally identified as the driving force of activity. The subsidiary values and beliefs that stemmed from this powerful statement developed and were absorbed into the very being of the heart of the school.

Getting the culture right

This too is a longer term strategy anticipated and expected by the leadership team. Having established the clear path and direction for the school, there came a period of approximately three years where these values and beliefs were tried and tested. Any institution will have its own atmosphere and ethos, and so too did St John's. Processes, activities and systems that have worked well in other places at other times had to be modified and moulded to fit the 'St John's way'. This concept took the new Headteacher some time to fully appreciate, and there was inevitably tension in the organization until acceptance and understanding was fully achieved. By the same token, it also took the staff and the student's time to settle and adapt to the new ideas.

The most important aspect of the new structure was the concept of *collegiality*. The aim of the new structure was to create a value driven model of collegiality which permeated throughout the staff structure making all members of staff feel part of the decision making process, more accountable to each other and making decision making easier and more diffuse throughout. As professionals we are all equal, have an equal voice and are trusted. Embedding this change took time, especially creating the belief that it was actually OK to take risks and that your voice was equal to that of anyone else in the organization. The underlying ethos shift had an impact across the school in terms of positive student attitudes, improving results and a willingness on the part of staff to embrace change.

By trial and error, experimentation and implementation of new initiatives, the culture was honed and fashioned towards its intended final position. There was a time of uncomfortableness for all client groups, staff, students, parents and governors alike while it settled down. By 2001 however the stability and direction was fixed and the school was ready to take on the major initiative of the 'Alternative Curriculum'.

During the next three years the teaching staff had been prepared by exposure to a constant range of initiatives connected with the child-centred focus. This too created tensions and led to complaints of 'too many initiatives, too often with little chance of consolidation.' Slowly over the three year period the teaching staff began to accept the increased pressure to take more responsibility for the learning of the students and recognize that the students themselves were capable, given the right encouragement, to take responsibility for their own learning. There was a strong move towards the philosophy as noted by Bosher and Hazlewood (2005: p. 121) 'If the child cannot learn the way you teach, can you teach the way the child learns?'

The school asked itself the question many times, 'have we got this right?' Quality control measures such as asking students how they felt about their learning, about teaching strategies they experienced, about their preferred learning styles and an analysis of external examination results began to give a positive picture. Additionally, parental surveys at parent's evenings, parent forums and open evenings began to show the positive effects these changes were having on the school. The teaching staff were also constantly being asked for their opinions and for constructive comments on progress being made.

Having achieved something like the desired culture for the school, the next question was how to maintain it. Constant reaffirmation of the core values and beliefs, and constant professional development opportunities which reinforced those values was the way forwards. Chime Communications publish and reinforce their core values and beliefs on a monthly basis via internal newsletters and emails, Syngenta constantly reaffirm their mission statement, targets and goals by ensuring that all written information used by the company to its workforce use a language which is easily understood by all, and confirms what the business is about.

It could not rest there though. As well as the staff, the wider community including the parents also needed constant reinforcement. This was achieved by school documentation containing the values, beliefs and mission statement, public reminders at all school / parents evening and meetings, and by means of electronic mail and school newsletters. Syngenta, Crown Lift Trucks and Chime Communications similarly maintain their values, belief message and mission statement through comparable workforce and client group meetings, and electronic publication transmittance of various kind.

Appointing the right workforce

Having changed the culture in the organization, created a set of values and beliefs that all members of the workforce understands , subscribes to and agrees to abide by, the initial task is almost complete. Once mechanisms are established to monitor, evaluate and reinforce those values, the next important step is to manage the workforce.

From experience, it is essential for the workforce that the leadership team is very clear about what is required for each post in the structure and more importantly what their position as employees is if there is a radical change in job role or title. If redundancies are likely, these need to be considered, costed and managed by the leadership team. This needs to be done prior to the launch of a new staffing structure. A management strategy or action plan must be established in preparation for potential unrest or tensions from the workforce.

In a new structure existing workers can then be either allocated to equivalent job roles, or if there is competition for promoted or different posts, some form of selection activities for example interviews need to be held.

With major restructuring, it does give the organization an opportunity to reallocate posts and positions, and employers need to be aware of this and be brave. It is an opportunity to appoint up and coming staff, staff with new ideas or with particular skills into the new positions. There must always be the caveat of keeping the workforce informed and aware of what is happening and why. This prevents misunderstandings which can lead to resentment, obstruction or outright lack of co-operation and loss of good will.

It may be that the SLT or the employers feel that a probationary period or trial period for the new post holders is appropriate. If this is the case, it must be stated at the start of the appointment process. Together with this, the length of the trial period and the process by which positions will either be confirmed as permanent or how a new selection processes will be organized need to be made public.

Once all posts are filled, trial periods completed and posts confirmed as permanent, the real task starts. All staff need to be motivated, continuously trained, retrained and encouraged. The best form of motivation is the personal satisfaction of doing a job well. All teaching staff are professionals with high academic qualifications. They enjoy mental stimulation and the autonomy of their work in the classroom. Thanks and recognition of a job well done is seen by most teachers as sufficient motivation to continue to work hard. A black mark for many schools develops out of this personal autonomy on occasions. Public recognition is not as frequently given as it should be in many institutions which bring seething resentment. This is the most corrosive of feelings for the leadership of a happy organization and such feelings can alter the morale of the workforce very quickly. Financial rewards are not as common in teaching as in other commercial areas. Many of the companies mentioned in this chapter offer financial incentive schemes and bonuses. Syngenta have a bonus system in place based on the achievement of personal targets and goals set as part of the appraisal cycle. Chime Communications operate an annual award scheme for which all employees are eligible to compete.

St John's does not have the financial flexibility to offer such schemes, but there is always the opportunity to enhance personal career development portfolios for future promotions and for many that is sufficient motivation.

In all organizations it is crucial that some form of motivational activity is undertaken by the leadership team on a regular basis. It must be fair, consistent and the workforce must recognize it as being appropriate and worthwhile. If this mechanism is in place, a motivated, contented and productive happy workforce will give their best to the organization.

In a summary to this section, Figure 2.3 identifies the strategies and actions required to bring about change.

Professionals in the institution

Professionalism is a theme throughout this book, and we elucidate different aspects of professionalism for different purposes.

Following on from the appointment of the right staff to the right posts and positions, for the teaching professional there is the added aspect of professionalism. Much has been written about professionalism and *The Concise Oxford Dictionary* (*COD*) (Pearsall 1999: p. 1140) defines the term professional as 'a paid occupation involving training and a formal qualification'. Teachers have long understood that they belonged to the 'profession' of teaching as it complies with the definition of the *COD* but Lawn and Ozga (1988) were concerned in 1988 about the 'proletarianization' of the teaching profession. Teachers had been under criticism for much of the 1980s and the respect hitherto afforded to them by the general public had reached alow ebb following the union unrest in the late 1970s. Lawn and Ozga (1988) felt that at the best, teachers were 'semi-professionals' in the eyes of the public as compared with other professional organizations like law or medicine. Darling-Hammond and Goodwin (1993: p. 19) in America also shared the concerns about 'the quasi professional status of teaching' and Goodlad (1990) referred to the 'not quite profession'.

To help the situation, in 1998 the General Teaching Council was formed by the government and this began to legitimise the 'Teaching Profession'. The General Teaching Council for England (the GTC) is the professional body for teaching in England

Action	Target group/s
Leader has an established clear vision	Outlined to the senior leaders
Ideas and concepts of the vision discussed	Strategic Leadership Team (SLT)
Analysis of existing cultural and ethos within the organisation	Undertaken by SLT
Decisions made on desired cultural context	Leader and SLT
Workforce and client groups informed of change intentions	Leader
Changes to existing mission statement	Leader plus SLT plus workforce
Changes to environment	Leader plus SLT plus workforce
Changes to values and beliefs	Leader plus SLT plus workforce
Changes to staffing and leadership structure	Leader plus SLT plus workforce
Any possible redundancy issues need to be planned, costed and managed prior to release to the workforce	SLT, financial leader and senior leader
Draft final working model of change revealed to workforce and client groups for consultation	Leader and SLT
Monitoring and evaluation of model undertaken	SLT and workforce
Modification as made as necessary	Leader, SLT and workforce
Final model confirmed	Workforce client groups, Governors or Board
Staffing model based on new culture developed	Leader and SLT
New job specifications developed	SLT plus workforce in collaboration
Appropriate staff appointed to relevant positions	Leader and SLT
New organizations operated for finite time before re-evaluation and quality control	Monitored by appropriate persons or groups within the system
New environment in place and running efficiently	Monitored by appropriate persons or groups within the system

Figure 2.3 An organization's summary checklist guide to a planned change of culture and staffing

and was established by the Teaching and Education Council 1998 which had two aims: 'to contribute to improving standards of teaching and the quality of learning, and to maintain and improve standards of professional conduct among teachers, in the interests of the public'.

The formation of the council legitimized the profession; it satisfied the earlier criticisms of a lack of occupational status, authority for self-governance and control over the membership by putting these features into its operating brief. These were all features undertaken by the more established professions giving them public acceptance and credibility.

Other professionals, it was noted by Lomax (1999: p. 12), formed a more traditional definition of professionalism as 'a measurement against type'. She noted:

> The institutionalised knowledge of the classical model was an example of the monopolisation of knowledge, with a club of experts based in universities who decided what could be counted or not. There is a general agreement that this approach was too elitist and that today all professional stakeholders should be involved in deciding the professional base of teaching.

Bosher (2001: p. 9) indicated a preference for a wider approach to the definition by saying 'teachers and pupils should have the opportunity to contribute to the knowledge base in which they are engaged'. The development of professionalism should be a dialogue between people with healthy and constructive disagreement on occasions. Lomax and Whitehead (1998: p. 12) point out: 'Professionalism is a process with a dialectical rather than a consensual basis. Constrained disagreement could be a productive basis for action . . . Constrained disagreement implies both critique and collaboration.'

This concept of dialectic between individuals is an important start to the conversation about teaching and professionalism. Teaching professionals have a moral responsibility and an accountability to their clients, the students and parents that overrides financial advantage or political ambition and professional status. It is the teachers' skill of being reflective and able to amend and alter the delivery of their specific subject knowledge to suit the client's needs that raises teaching skills above those of being a craft or job to professional status.

At St John's there is a leadership expectation that all members of the teaching staff will exhibit the highest standard of professional behaviour. That is, outstanding subject knowledge, appropriate teaching qualifications and experience, appropriate dress which adheres to the code laid down by the school and professional relationships with colleagues and client groups. There is also an expectation of vocational dedication rather than tasks completed for pecuniary advantage. This is the ideal, but St John's like any other organization is full of people which by definition means that there are differences in interpretation of professionalism, different degrees of conformity to that interpretation and adherence to the concept. It is incumbent of the Headteacher, the head leader and his SLT to ensure that the standards that have been established are adhered to or sanction action taken. It is also incumbent on the leadership to ensure that the required standards and expectations are explained to every employee on appointment and constantly reinforced to all the members of the organization.

Assuming these conditions are established and operating, the school or organization can then get about its core business secure in the knowledge of quality assurance. It can accept for instance that in the professional framework environment there can be clear and honest conversations between individuals as equals, each respecting the other's point of view. This can only enhance the quality of outcome for the organization as a whole and for the clients. To extend this concept further, if contributions made by equals are valued, there should be no limit to the overall vision of the organization. Each individual is free to contribute to the process of developing new ideas, concepts and strategies with the ultimate aim of organizational improvement. A professional team is of enormous value to the organization. If the core values and beliefs are understood and adhered to, and the core purpose of the organization delivered in an efficient and effective manner by a well qualified and experienced staff, the organization will inevitably thrive and be successful. Syngenta, Chime, Click Tools and Crown Lift Trucks all make a specific point of ensuring that all employees regardless of their position in the various companies all have access to senior management, and that senior management is prepared to listen to and act upon ideas which have been generated at any point in the company.

The final word on professionalism has to be addressed to members of the workforce that have no 'professional training' or qualifications. In an institution like St John's, half the workforce is comprised of support staff in a variety of different roles and job specifications. While they do not fall under the agreed definition of professional, the organization could not operate without them. As part of the leadership approach, these employees deserve equal recognition, praise and motivation in order to make their contribution to the success of the organization.

This is an issue that will be raised in Chapter 3 because St John's failed and is still failing to address this fully. The consequence of which is to have a dissatisfaction and tension permeating through the organization which is counterproductive.

3 Managing change

The management structures and the way they changed over time

The start of this chapter is a step back in time. In Chapter 1, the current staffing and leadership structure at St John's School has been described in detail together with how the individuals within the structure coalesce to make it an effective collegiate body. To allow the reader to get a feel of how the current structure was reached, there is a commentary here of the changes associated with the positioning of the staff of the school to reach towards the goal of education in the twenty-first century.

It is interesting to reflect on Hopkins et al. (1994: p. 4) historical perspective on the influences to changes in education.

> Some twenty years or so ago 'change' was about working with new curriculum materials prepared by national or local agencies. Or it may have meant trying out a new teaching strategy. Most of these changes were ad hoc, self determined, single innovations which by and large individual teachers decided to work on, or not, as the case might be. More recently we have not had the luxury of choice. In the UK as elsewhere, the change agenda has increasingly been set by national politicians, rather than being advocated by educationalists or support agencies. With the centralisation of educational reform, teachers have lost control over change.

Since that passage was written, the centralization of education has continued remorselessly. Not all of those actions should be viewed negatively however, and the allusion to changes in curriculum content has been addressed at a local level in many schools with the inclusion of a skills based curriculum as noted in Bosher and Hazlewood (2005).

This increased the activities of the teachers in classrooms developing their own teaching strategies and resources to address this new and different way of learning for students. What became clear is that as the century drew to a close the National Curriculum introduced in 1988 was becoming redundant for life in the twenty-first century.

In many ways, while one could take issue with the centralized control of education by the Government because of its narrow perspectives on what could and should be taught to the next generation of adults, this centralization has achieved a focus and motivation for educational development. It has encouraged teachers to become more focused on their field of expertise, the processes of teaching and learning. What Hopkins et al. (1994) noted was that teacher's involvement in initiatives of any kind until recently has been variable and random in direction, involvement and quality. Some would argue for this as a positive situation, with teachers investigating and implementing issues that were of professional interest to them and the students under their care. While this is commendable, it is the randomness of the situation that causes a problem. Under such a system, there is no guarantee that all students in one school, let alone nationally or internationally will all have the same experiences and all receive the benefits which might accrue from such initiatives. This is not an argument for the national control of educational systems experienced in many Asian countries like China and South Korea and in France where each lesson is delivered at the same time in all schools. It is however an observation that teachers are very good at 'reinventing wheels' and in the process, wasting valuable time and resources. What centralization gave was a focus on specific areas for research and development that would benefit all students in all schools. There is an issue of quality control over what is being developed to ensure students are not to suffer as guinea pigs in an educational experiment, but rigorous monitoring and evaluation at local level can eradicate this as a problem.

What really becomes the key area for development is the concept of moving an individual school or the national educational system forwards. This forward movement has to come from informed, experienced and visionary leaders at local and national level. For an institution or an organization to plateau, born out of lack of vision, lack of courage, laziness or complacency is to go backwards in development.

Chapter 1 of *Nurturing Independent Thinkers* (Bosher and Hazlewood 2005: p. 9) pointed to the danger of complacency at organizational and national levels when measuring success. Whether it is for an internal reorganization or a national educational initiative, an objective view is required. In both education and in business, there is a need for organizations to stop and analyse where they are, what they stand for and where they are going. *The danger comes in the replication of the measure for success when the world around has moved on and what made the organization successful may no longer be sufficient to maintain the upward trend. This phenomenon is as true of education as it is for business and industrial organizations.*

It is not the complacency itself which is so detrimental to the organization, but the mindset of the organization's leaders who cannot or do not see the changes taking place around them. The consequence of this inactivity is the loss of productivity and position in the market place.

Chapter 1 also noted that the National Curriculum developed in 1998, had become redundant by the end of the century and a new and breathtaking approach to learning, the curriculum and teaching pedagogue was required for the new millennium. The goal posts had changed, and education needed to change with them in order to support the needs of industry, commerce, business and society.

If it is accepted that change is an imperative to maintain a competitive edge at individual and national levels, then organizations must grasp the nettle and do it. Lavié (2006), in his discourse on teacher collaboration was right to identify the root of excellence in schools. He said: 'School excellence is the result of a rational planning process supported by the Principal's leadership, whose actions encourage vision building processes, set the tone of the school, and shape in many ways, the organisational conditions in which teachers work.'

Cognizant of this ideal, the Headteacher and the Strategic Leadership Team at St John's set about the process of structural and management change.

Chapter 1 showed how St John's became involved in the delivery of a new curriculum initiative which in turn necessitated changes to the management structure of the teaching staff which in turn necessitated development of a different structure for support staff. Change from what to what? Since 1997, the school has undertaken successive series of significant changes to its management structure, and this section will document

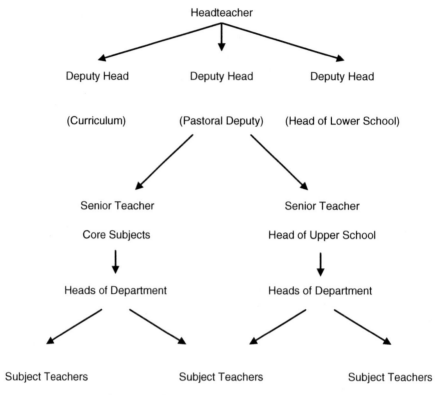

Figure 3.1 The management structure in 1996

those changes. In 1996, the staffing structure for the school was a very conventional hierarchical management model as shown in Figure 3.1.

This management model was traditional and because of its hierarchical structure, decision making, decision taking and the movement of information up and down the structure was slow. In small schools or organizations this may be sufficient for mediocre effectiveness. As soon as the organization increases in size and internal complexity, this becomes a very inefficient model, and because of its autocracy, members in the organization are deskilled at the decision taking and making processes. With those restrictions in mind, the new Headteacher to the school created a new staffing and management structure to improve efficiency and effectiveness.

This began with the simple repositioning of a central value, the child. It is a statement of the obvious, but what is often lost in schools is that the centre of all endeavours must be the child, and every day that the child spent in school mattered. Therefore, the most important relationship in the school was that between teacher and child. If this was to be effective then the primary function of those with managerial responsibility was to support this relationship and put it above all other considerations. In the prevailing jargon this entailed a 'flattening of the hierarchy'. The school moved to one Deputy Headteacher with three Assistant Headteachers and the management 'pyramid' inverted (Murgatroyd & Morgan 1993). The Bursar and Headteacher's Personal Assistant joined the management team, now referred to as the Strategic Management Team.

Three curriculum schools were formed: the School of Culture, the School of Sciences and the School of Personal Development, and these schools were managed by the Assistant Headteachers. The most important aspect of the new structure was the concept of *collegiality* (see Chapter 4). As professionals all staff are all equal, have an equal voice and are trusted. In the decision making process the Directors' role was to represent the Directorate and their views as a collective position. Embedding this change in took time; especially creating the belief that it was actually permissible to take risks and that your voice was equal to that of anyone else in the organization. The underlying ethos shift had an impact across the school in terms of creating positive student attitudes, improving results and a willingness on the part of staff to embrace change. It was in this context that the Curriculum for the 21st Century (The Integrated Curriculum) was introduced.

Between 1997 and the introduction of the Integrated Curriculum in 2001, the leadership team in the school continued to refine the model seen in Figure 3.2 to continually improve effectiveness and efficiency. What the new structure gave to the staff in the organization was an opportunity to take more and additional responsibilities and to offer an increased range of professional development opportunities.

An important spin-off from this structure occurred with the encouragement of the Headteacher and leadership staff. The traditional closed classroom door and the security that this brought to teachers was opened. Team teaching, peer observations and shared groups slowly became the norm. After some initial apprehensions, the St John's staff soon embraced these new practices. In line with research in the area, staff quickly valued the Continuing Professional Development (CPD) that the structure offered. Boyle, Wilde and Boyle (2004: p. 45) noted: 'The most popular longer term professional

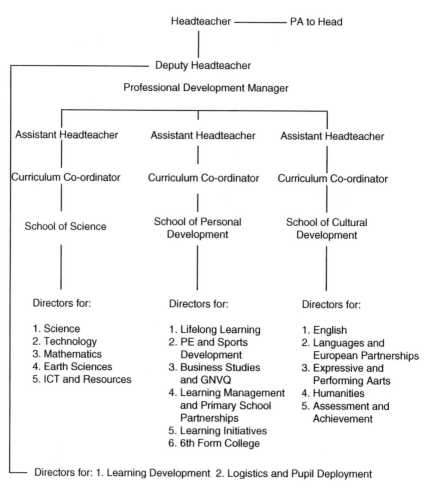

Figure 3.2 The management structure in September 1997

development activities (that were also generally rated as being of good quality by the participant) were the observations of colleagues and the sharing of practice.'

Boyle et al. (2004: p. 46) went onto to confirm: 'The continual deepening of knowledge and skills is an integral part of the development of any professional working in any profession. One important means of achieving competitive advantage is the creation of conditions for the rapid acquisition of new knowledge and skills.'

The culture was changing and the teaching staff were up-skilling themselves by working in a more collegiate manner than before. The issue of collegiality will be discussed in detail in Chapter 4, but these preparatory changes were paving the way for future development. This was not accidental, but a planned leadership strategy by the Headteacher.

Direct comparative strategies can be envisaged for other types of organizations, flattening the hierarchy, developing and motivating the staff by increased Continuing Professional Development and developing professional autonomy was putting the 'feel good factor' into the workforce.

As recognized in Chapter 2, to accommodate this new thinking a cultural shift had to be accomplished from the child being the 'product' (Handy 1994) manipulated by adults in the institution, to a position where the child was at the centre of all that the organization did and stood for. A diagrammatic representation of the child centred model can be seen as Figure 3.3.

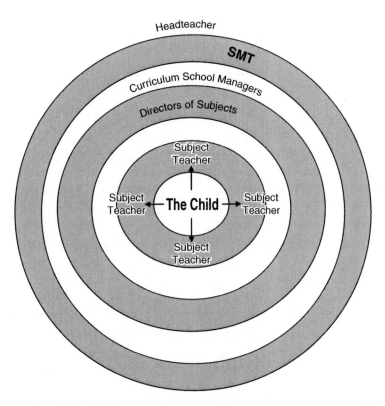

Figure 3.3 The relationship between the new staff management structure and the child

Figure 3.3 shows the management structure from a child-centred perspective in 2001. The flow chart in Chapter 2 of the Syngenta model is very similar in as much as the core values and product are at the centre of all corporate activity with the top and bottom of the organization feeding into this central concept. Thus it is possible for most organizations of different kinds to adopt the same principle in their approach.

With this modified structure in place, the school was able to establish and maintain the new approach to the curriculum which over the intervening years had developed into a significant organization in the school. This process was not without its problems, and these will be discussed later in the chapter.

The school has always prided itself on being a dynamic forward looking innovative institution. In 2005, an external change agent stimulated a further modification and sophistication to the model.

The change agent was the Government initiative led by the Secretary of State for Education which set out to remodel the incentive and management allowances for teachers. The deliberations at Government level started in 2002 under the direction of Estelle Morris, then Secretary of State for Education and came on stream in the summer of 2005.

The Teaching and Learning Responsibilities (TLRs) guidance received from the Government was reviewed by the School Teachers Review Body (STRB) in February 2005, agreed by the Secretary of State for Education in May and was projected to come into force from 1 January 2006. The change was focused on the way teachers were able to receive additional payments and responsibilities. Hitherto, the Headteacher of a school could reward a teacher with responsibility points (Management Allowances – MAs) for undertaking any form of extra work or managerial responsibility in the individual school. This award was under the direct control of the Headteacher and the Governing body. Following the TLR implementation, such financial and promotional awards had to be directly associated with teaching and learning, the criteria for which was dictated centrally. The only criteria for the award of a TLR post were:

- Impact on educational progress beyond the teachers' assigned pupils
- Leading, developing and enhancing the teaching of others

- Having accountability for leading, developing and enhancing a subject or curriculum area or pupil development across the curriculum
- Having line management responsibility for a significant number of people

With these strict criteria in place, the Headteacher at St John's saw an opportunity to radically change the historical staffing and leadership structure of the school. The plans for the TLR changes had been in the public domain for several years, and the SLT had, under the leadership of the Headteacher been looking at a number of different staffing models which would do two things. First, the model had to be in line with the Governments plans. Secondly, the vision for the future of the school needed a radical change and this provided the opportunity.

The Headteacher's vision was for a workforce that had a great degree of individual autonomy and freedom in its action and decision making. At the same time, it was expected that roles and posts were very flexible and would constantly overlap. With this very flexible model in place, it should allow for the person best qualified for a particular task to make decisions and undertake implementation. By qualified, this is not just in the academic sense, but in terms of appropriate experience, previous involvement with similar initiatives or tasks, or simply having sufficient time to complete the job. To achieve this, many barriers had to be overcome and old fashioned thinking and prejudice put aside. This structure depended on all members of the team working in a collegiate manner, a massive change from the historical individual autonomy of teachers. It also required a cultural change in the way subjects were to be taught, delivered and managed.

Traditionally organizations have a diagram of accountability and line management described earlier in the chapter. For a fully collegiate organization this is not so easy to describe diagrammatically. Figure 1.5 may help in understanding with the following aide memoir. Overlaps indicate a 'working together' expectation although the circle describes the individual teams. The over-arching (remember it's a circle) parts show that these teams will be involved throughout the organization on a needs / demand basis – they can appear at any time and in any place.

In an attempt to describe the final Strategic Leadership Team agreed model to the staff in a way that they could understand the thinking, Figure 1.5 was used. The model is fully explained in Chapter 1 and so will not be repeated here, but the issues surrounding its development and inception are the focus for the next part of this chapter.

Managing the change process – a new staffing structure

In this section, a view will be taken from both sides of the coin regarding the management of change. It does not matter what sort of establishment or institution is involved in change, the perspectives will be very similar, as will the thought process of both the employees and the leadership teams. From the leader's point of view, it is imperative that he or she understands the likely pitfalls that can occur through lack of knowledge, sensitivity or experience in dealing with the fragile, fraught and often emotional issues that accompany change. If these can be anticipated, resolved or action planned in advance, the process of change becomes less problematic. To that end, let us first examine the mindset and thought processes that can go through the employee's minds when faced with the possibility of change. These concerns will provide definite barriers to the change process unless there is agreed and amicable settlement by employees and the leadership team.

An employee's perspective

From an employee's point of view how does all this change feel? It does not matter whether it is a school staff or a commercial organization, it is the workforce that really holds the power to help or obstruct when change is being undertaken. Does the leadership team really understand this and acknowledge the power 'behind the throne'?

Looking from the inside out at the change process can give a salutary view of the organization, and perhaps more leaders should do this more often. So how does it feel, what are the major concerns, what will convince me as an employee to take on board and support the proposed changes from the leadership team? This section is written intentionally in the first person. I would express the following concerns:

- 'will I still have a job?' A detailed look at Figure 1.5 of the St John's school leadership innovation shows a completely new approach and a change to conventional structure which is beyond the experience of the workforce. The commonly accepted names and easily understood hierarchical positions of the management structure have disappeared, 'where am I?'

- 'will I still have the same status, responsibility and financial reward as I did under the old structure? If not then I cannot support the change, I have worked hard for what I enjoy at present'.
- 'are others perhaps younger, less experienced or in my view less able than I being promoted above and around me?'
- 'what do you expect me to do under the new structure that is different to what I do now, are you expecting me to work harder or longer or both?'
- 'who will manage me?'
- 'will I have to work harder?'

It will depend on the satisfactory response to these questions as to how co-operative I am to the change process. Ultimately, the final solution if I am dissatisfied is for me to leave the organization. However, this is a 'council of last resort' both for me and for the organization itself. Negotiated compromise if necessary would be the more positive way forwards.

Additional barriers to proposed structural management change

The leadership team must also take other potential barriers to the proposed change into consideration and manage them out of the equation if success is to be achieved. Again a list of questions to be addressed:

Concerns at internal, local and national levels

- Can the organization afford the proposed changes within the budget, is it catered for in the organizations projected business plan?
- If there is overstaffing in a particular area that leads to redundancy of expertise, how does the management propose to deal with this?
- Are there sufficient facilities to accommodate the new proposals, particularly if for instance, more office space is required?
- Is there sufficient administrative support in place to accommodate the servicing of the new structure?
- Does the new structure require additional or different expertise to that provided by the existing team?
- If new expertise is needed, what is the recruiting plan, with dates set and a clear view of what or who is required?
- For all the proposed changes is there a clear job specification which is published in a manner and a language which is easily understood by the workforce and all the client groups affected by the change?

- Are there Continuing Professional Development implications for the change?
- Do training activities need to be undertaken prior to the implementation of the change?
- Has the 'roll out date' for the change or initiative been clearly publicized?
- Are the stakeholder groups aware of the impending change, do they understand it and do they understand the role they are to play in the process? Do these proposals affect stakeholders in any significant way? In an educational setting I am thinking of groups like Governors or parents. In the commercial setting it may be subsidiary companies, component suppliers, other service suppliers or partners in other countries. For example, HSBC Bank have gone to considerable lengths to ensure that all members of both the workforce and the customer base are clear that there are different cultural, ethical and work practice expectations in operation in its branches in different countries across the globe. It is essential that any leadership decisions made take these differences into consideration in the efforts to produce agreement and harmony.
- Is the proposed change in line with local and national initiatives and structures?

The leadership perspective

Some important decisions have to be made by the leadership team. Decisions about possible changes in staffing numbers, the possibility of redundancy and how to manage that, and the sufficiency of financial resources post the change should be first in the discussions. It is essential that all the employees concerns are addressed in an organized and logical fashion if the result is to be positive and reassuring. Time is always of the essence, and the overall project should be timed so that there is no overt rush to implementation, but that the intermediate consultative stages are successfully managed and clear and unambiguous information communication is undertaken at all stages.

Using St John's as an example, the following stages were undertaken: Two years prior to the implementation date in 2005, the Headteacher had a number of meetings with the Strategic Leadership Team to establish some models of possible structural configurations which may accommodate the educational vision of the Headteacher.

This vision was to establish a leadership structure of teaching staff that operated in a fully collegiate manner for all aspects of the professional job of teaching young people. The development of the concept of 'collegiality' and of its extension 'radical collegiality' is the focus of Chapter 4, but the process of establishing a collegial environment will be discussed here. Leadership from the Headteacher was required to alter the team mindset from the existing flattened hierarchical model in place to the 'collegiate model' for the future. Even at senior leadership level, members of the team were initially reluctant to subscribe to the concept without a clear view of what it entailed and what the implications were. All members of the senior team were in the same position as the 'employee' example described earlier in the chapter with all the concomitant worries about position, status and pay.

The central figure as the child was re-emphasized, and all activities and structures were to radiate from this centrality as described in Figure 3.3. The other significant feature of the new plan was that there should be a continuation of the work started with the Alternative Curriculum described in *Nurturing Independent Thinkers* (Bosher & Hazlewood 2005). This skill based, rather than the conventional content led curriculum, required a different professional approach. It was started as a small scale project for Year 7 students in 2001, but as they moved through the school, there became a clear requirement to re-orientate the staffing structure to allow freedom for this organic model to develop and grow. The brief was, in concise terms, a child-centred, skill based curriculum with a collegiate staffing structure.

Once the design brief was set, the models to accommodate it started to be discussed. The Strategic Team of seven, five of whom had at least 15 years of teaching experience, slowly started to evolve structures for consideration. The range and wealth of experience is noted here because it was essential that workable pragmatic ideas were considered, not evangelical 'pie in the sky' evolutions which probably looked good on paper but were practically infeasible. Slowly the picture started to be drawn. It was a progressive and risky move of leadership to throw away the managerial conventions of the past years of education and start with a blank canvas.

There were several sticking points that led to substantial discussion. It started with terminology. If the new structure was to encompass new areas and responsibilities, new terminology was required which appropriately described the roles the new posts fulfilled. Here is where the difficulties started. It is relatively easy to formulate new titles for posts, much more difficult to achieve the appropriate balance of job description and relative status. With the conventional ideas of posts like Head of Department, the concept was so ingrained in teacher's minds that they knew exactly what the job entailed and the relative seniority that was attached to that post. Use a new term like *Phase Progression Leader* and that comfort of understanding disappears. What also disappears is the formal power base of the individual. Teachers rarely talk about 'power', but it is there and implied in terms of who has influence over whom and where any one individual appears in the 'pecking order' in the institution. These concerns must not be overlooked in importance. Leadership and Managerial posts must carry the mantle of seniority within their titles if they are to be treated with the gravitas that the post holders require, and the workforce reacts to. The battle of semantics commenced.

Concomitant with the new terminology were the new job descriptions. It was not anticipated to start with how important to the change process these descriptions were. Again at senior level, absolute clarity of job role was required in order to make sense of the overall vision. The process engaged in was a transformational one. It was transmitting the vision of the Headteacher into a practical every day environment. For the workforce, job descriptions became the 'be all and end all'. For the future, a lesson learnt was the need for a clear matrix of the interrelationships between each component in the system, and an explanatory composite diagram such as Figure 1.5. This was lacking in the management strategy at St John's for a long time and brought a number of barriers into play as a result.

Over the course of many Strategic Leadership Team meetings and conferences, the staffing pattern started to emerge. Members of Strategic Leadership Team, in an unplanned way, took on the mantle of playing 'devil's advocate' to propositions suggested by the remainder of the team. This proved to be a healthy and positive way forwards; the 'what if' scenario was played many times with members of the team postulating solutions. Eventually the draft plan was formed, the possible redundancy issue addressed and the action plan for dealing with staff that no longer quite fitted the new configuration agreed. The time scale for this activity took about a year of constant modelling and remodelling.

Restructuring in an educational setting is not the sole preserve of this country. Much work on restructuring by Elmore (1990) and Murphy (1991) in America was based on the work of the Carnegie Forum (1986) report *Teachers for the 21st Century* and the Holmes Group report (1986). These reports provided the bedrock for an enormous amount of research from which the American Educational system started to make plans for how it was to operate in the twenty-first century. They provide a useful comparative tool against which to measure the pitfalls and difficulties entailed in managing restructuring change. Elmore (1990) on the back of this research emphasized that in any restructuring activity, superficial tinkering with items like the budget on their own would not bring about the desired changes for the organization. A deeper and more substantial approach was required. He confirmed that the components for a successful restructuring process must involve three elements.

- Changing the way teaching and learning occurs in schools
- Changing the organization and internal features of schools, the so called 'workplace conditions'
- Changing the distribution of power between the school and its clients

Elmore in Hopkins et al. (1994: p. 17) went on to argue that unless all three of these components were in place and addressed, there would be little improvement in efficiency or effectiveness of outcome in performance for the school.

The restructuring process at St John's followed these guidelines both in detail and in depth. The results are still to be recognized as the system needs to 'bed in' and settle into a working format. Early analysis shows improvement for the students in both performance and in terms of providing a 'rounded' educational experience for the students. For the teaching staff, the situation is starting to show benefits. The quality assurance research put in places as a necessary part of the monitoring process (Bosher 2008) records that many more teachers in the second year of operation are now feeling the liberating influence of the new structure. Liberating in terms of allowing the individual to make their own decisions , anticipate the students needs and satisfy them, and devise appropriate teaching strategies which are in sympathy with the preferred learning styles of the students.

The implementation process

Such radical change does not happen by chance or overnight. Much preparatory work has to be undertaken by the Senior Leadership Team, and by the middle leaders. Where did it start?

The genesis came with the appointment of the Assistant Head Teachers who were to lead the Curriculum Schools. In an agreed democratic manner, the job descriptions for all parts of the new structure were advertised as internal posts and applicants were encouraged to consider their preferences and experience and apply formally for interview. This process in turn was carried out for positions throughout the new structure. One of the strengths of this overt process was that it gave all teaching employees opportunities for career enhancement and professional development opportunities to posts which hitherto had been unavailable to them. It created the opportunity of movement and promotion for developing 'rising stars'. With a very few exceptions, applications made were appropriately for the level of expertise and experience of the applicants and they were then interviewed. For those who made too ambitious an application, they received encouragement and careers counselling to direct them towards training opportunities which would in the future enable them to apply successfully for the posts advertised. One important principle adopted early in this change process was to start with a blank sheet as far as posts and present staff were concerned. There was a danger and a great temptation to fit the current staff into the new positions. Personalities start to take over the thinking process, and before long inappropriate decisions may be made based on poor thinking about the current staffing population. The important priority was to find the right person to fit the post so that new thinking and dynamism was introduced into the equation. If the established workforce had just been moved across, little new thinking would have occurred.

The Strategic Leadership Team spent a considerable amount of time considering the person specification for each role. The team also reviewed the requisite skills, experience and approach needed for a successful appointment. While the matrix of Belbin's Team Role Theory in West (1994) was not followed explicitly, the sound sense of creating teams composed of members with complementary skills was an option which was considered to be very important. Following the appointment of the Assistant Headteachers, a minute from a Strategic Leadership Team conference of 18 June 2007 reads, 'one of the primary objectives of the conference is for the Assistant Headteachers to gain a full understanding of their remit and the management of the Curriculum Schools'.

Once this group had been briefed and were aligned with their roles and responsibilities, the next phase of the implementation process could commence. This was for the appointment of different layers of posts within the planned new structure (see Figure 1.5). For each post, a full job description was available. This application and appointment process was backed up by a series of staff meetings where the overall structure and the individual job roles were explained in detail.

From Figure 1.5, it is clear that there are numerous teams involved in a complex interrelationship keeping the child at the centre of operations. As each team member was appointed, they were involved by the Strategic Leadership Team in appointing the next members of the team. The reader should remember that this structure is circular not hierarchical, so ideas of seniority were an issue that is discussed later.

Eventually, all team places were filled, and under the ethos of the collegiate working model to be discussed in Chapter 4 they set about action planning for their team operation.

Barriers to implementation

Having identified the employees perceptions earlier in the chapter, all of those concerns could be considered as barriers to the successful launch of the new structure. The key concerns regarding pay and status were the most important to resolve early. The pay issue under the new Teaching and Learning Responsibilities guidance (2006) was relatively easy to overcome. Each of the new posts embraced the spirit of the regulations and so staff would not be penalized. Careful staffing analysis of the new roles measured against the existing staffing complement was undertaken and the results showed that there was a need for some redundancy, but by and large, no significant staff loss was required. Those who faced possible redundancy were counselled individually; additionally, voluntary redundancy was offered to all members of staff who might be interested, and eventually a selection was made by the Headteacher. In the event, one person took voluntary redundancy, and others who were deemed redundant in one area offered their teaching expertise in other areas and the problem diminished. Having taken into consideration the caveat earlier of not appointing existing personnel into new positions, the selection process was designed to allow for fresh appointments and for career development for different teachers on the staff. To allow for fresh blood to develop the simple expedient of internal advertisement for all posts was undertaken and all members of staff were invited to apply if interested.

The major barrier to implementation was the lack of understanding by the majority of teaching staff on how the new system interlocked. The question of 'who will do this or that job in the new structure' occupied staff conversations for many months. The apparent process of removing status / power for established career teachers was not a battle won easily. Resolution did not come easily and two years on, the research analysis from Bosher (2008) still finds pockets of resistance in existence. The resolution to the lack of understanding was achieved by a concentrated series of small and large group meetings together with personal and team interviews given by the Headteacher.

There were and still are a small number of cynical critics of the system who will not accept or see the benefits that the new structure could bring. These people will exist in any organization, and it is up to the peer group and the Strategic Leadership Team between them to convince the few of the benefits that can be achieved. From a leadership perspective, these cynics need special focus from the Strategic Leadership Team. Depending on whom the cynic is, and their 'standing' in the organization, they can be destructive to any innovation. Therefore they do need to be harnessed into the positive thinking process as soon as possible. Other less solvable barriers were the physical ones. Insufficient office space, support staff and team teaching areas, were considerable impediments to the system. It required considerable inventiveness and lateral thinking on behalf of all staff to reach a negotiated compromise on these issues. Eventually working solutions were found and implemented.

Mistakes made

At this stage we will consider the role of 'mistakes', but argue that it is in part a defined strategy to aid collegial learning.

The major mistake made in the implementation of this restructuring project was the lack of clear communication about team and individual roles within the structure. The complete revolution of changing roles and job designation terminology was a step too far for most staff. While the Headteacher's philosophy was to allow teams to evolve and create their own identity under the banner of collegiality, this proved to be a difficult philosophy for staff to grasp. There was much protectionism undertaken to preserve status, or subject identity. This proved difficult to shake off for the leadership team. The best solution as it emerged was for the enthusiastic embracers of the new structure to work hard in a united way to convince the half-hearted or the doubters that there was workable merit in the new ideas.

The other mistake made was the judgement not to embrace the support staff in the school within the new structure. The support staff numbers had increased dramatically as a result of work place reform (DfES 2004), and the workforce complement now almost equalled that of the teaching staff. It was clearly, in hindsight, a mistake not to integrate this group within the structure. It antagonized and disenfranchised these colleagues from the decision making and development processes, just at a time when their expertise was the most needed.

Twelve lessons learnt

Are there lessons to be learnt from this process? The answer to this is yes, both for the case study institution and also for any organization undertaking a similar radical change in organizational structure.

- Given time, constant encouragement and reinforcement, the process works. If the philosophical ground on which the initiative is based is seen to be both sound and workable for the employees and the client base, it will work. The success may be slow in coming, but as more of the workforce becomes attuned to the idea, they become evangelical representatives of the ideal. Eventually a critical mass is reached, and slowly the doubters and cynics become the minority. From the client's point of view, Bosher (2008) found that the students themselves, while not being overtly aware of the restructuring process, did feel the impact of the change. They felt that their learning experience had improved offering the possibility of better examination and learning experiences.
- Communication and transparency are central to any initiatives success. Without a clear statement of vision, intent and method, suspicion and confusion result. Once doubts are formed, it takes much longer to bring about the transformation to a new and effective operation.
- All aspects of the induction and implementation process must be considered and action plans put in place before the initiative is revealed to the consumers. Financial implications, staffing levels and cuts, misplaced personnel, awkward job role fits all have to be anticipated and resolved before 'roll out'.
- The head of the organization has to be able to totally rely on his strategic leadership team to spread the same supportive message throughout the organization. Syngenta and Chime Communications both also recognize the importance of this in their strategy developments and continue to place great efforts on it in an ongoing basis to maintain sustainability.
- To maintain sustainability, constant reinforcement, clarification and reiteration of the message has to be made by all those in leadership roles.
- To recognize the power of peer group pressure. Active and strong support for the initiative by those who are involved in it is a great advertisement for success to those who are still in doubt.
- Active promotion and publicity of successes of individuals or groups within the system.

- Interrelated systems allow and encourage cross fertilization of ideas and resources which are valuable both in their own right and as the cement which binds the whole organization together.
- Ensure that all stake holders or client groups are at least aware of the development, but better still involved in the development and implementation of the process.
- Make sure that consultation and involvement of the staff is undertaken at as many stages as possible as the process develops. In that way, nothing appears as a surprise at the end, and the process becomes more understood and embedded with time.
- Visual representation of the final product makes understanding much easier than just words; for example, Figure 1.5.
- Put in place good quality control and monitoring measures in order that progress and success can be tracked. In addition, data from such monitoring processes enables the identification of trouble and allows for earlier remedial intervention.

At this point, the chapter has identified how the process of change in any organization might be approached. It has identified the steps to be undertaken and the process of implementation. It has looked at the proposed change from the leadership team perspective and from an employee's point of view, and recognized that both parties have concerns that must be addressed. It is important that any barriers to improvement are identified, recognized and removed if possible. This may be a slow process, but attrition of a positive nature over time is the way forwards.

4 Collegiality – a new paradigm

Collegiality is not a new concept but it is one that is capable of being misunderstood and misinterpreted. In terms of educational management it can be considered to be at one end of a spectrum in which hierarchical structures occupy the other end. The paradox of true collegiality in an educational system that emphasizes control and accountability was alluded to in Chapter 1. This chapter will explore collegiality as a concept and a leadership model for twenty-first century schools and colleges. It is one that will also be recognized in business and commercial sectors in part to a greater or lesser extent.

The world of education at the beginning of the twenty-first century is littered with a multitude of terms and ideas all seeking to bring about the holy grail of a high quality educational experience *for all*, with excellent qualification outcomes *for all* in a context of lifelong learning. The political intention to ensure that all learners remain in full time education to at least the age of 18 with over 50 per cent going on to University also recognizes that the way in which education has been viewed in the twentieth century no longer applies.

David Hargreaves' (2004) brief from the Specialist Schools and Academies Trust (SSAT) to explore personalized learning led to the creation of nine gateways (see Figure 4.1).

The nine gateways created a forum for debate among the profession who recognized that each gateway or theme was applicable to every school, every classroom and therefore all teaching and learning. The detailed exploration of these themes promoted by the SSAT led D. Hargreaves (2006) to develop four additional concepts or 'deeps' – Deep Learning, Deep Experience, Deep Support and Deep Leadership. This development recognized the complexity of relationship between the nine gateways and sought to focus debate at a deeper level, hence the title.

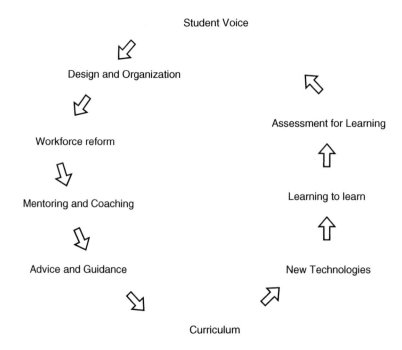

Figure 4.1 D. Hargreaves' (2004) nine gateways to personalized learning

Deep Learning reflected the position that all schools recognize which is that exams and results are only a part of their core purpose. Creating the conditions to allow learners to understand how to learn to learn, supporting their development towards becoming autonomous, self-motivated and resilient learners who could learn and re-learn at any stage of their lives is the deeper purpose of schooling. In terms of the gateways learning to learn, assessment for learning and the student voice were the key strands. Deep experience understood that the quality of interaction between teachers/staff and students, students and students and indeed teachers and teachers was at the centre of developing independent, confident, capable and responsible learners. Engaging students through the curriculum and new technologies was perceived to be intrinsically important. Deep support anticipated the needs of schools and learners that would be necessary for all participants if personalizing learning was to become a reality. Finally Deep Leadership concentrated on the transformation that would be necessary in leadership to bring about the transformation of schools (see Figure 4.2).

In developing an understanding of collegiality in the context of the work of Hargreaves and SSAT, it can be considered to flow through the nine 'gateways' and

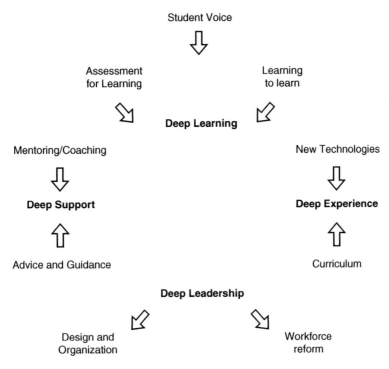

Figure 4.2 D. Hargreaves' four 'deeps'

four 'deeps'. Student voice, learning to learn, curriculum, mentoring and coaching, advice and guidance and leadership are all reflections of collegiality and collegiate practice but the reality is often far removed. How often is the experience of the student in school one of being told what to do, how to do, when to do? Can it really be otherwise? The teacher in position of control of both environment and knowledge is an established position. Accountable for quality of learning, quantitative outcomes and safety of those within his/her control, the teacher has few alternatives. Discipline in the learning environment is paramount; otherwise, anarchy and disaffection rise swiftly. So wither collegiality? Is it a philosopher's dream for a co-operative partnership between all in the classroom, in the school and further afield or is it pragmatically a nonsense?

Collegiality is defined in various ways but for the purpose of this discussion it can be described as 'a form of social organization based on shared and equal participation by all of its members'. It implies collective responsibility and describes a group of people united in common purpose who have respect for each others' abilities in working towards that purpose.

If we set aside the apparent paradox between collegiality and leadership for the time being, we can explore two aspects of the nine gateways. The Student Voice is central to allowing children to participate in their learning. Being able to express their views on the experiences of schooling is one part; knowing that they will be listened to and appropriate action in response to their views taken is quite another. The Student Voice discussed in educational circles sounds as though serious dialogue which directly impacts on learning is taking place. But is this the reality or does the term hide a schism in the collegiate aspiration? Cruddas (2007) identifies the distinction between adult and child that the term 'student voice' reinforces. The distinction between the two further reinforces the power relationship with the adult being in the ascendancy. It is perhaps a statement of the obvious that the teacher must have authority to maintain appropriate control and therefore the child cannot be a truly collegiate partner in the classroom. Cruddas' analysis is complex but compelling. She argues for the voices of adults and children to be 'engaged voices' leading to the construction of shared social meanings which lead 'imperfectly towards jointly conceived understandings of personhood and community' and 'reflect the kind of communities and the kind of world we want to live in'.

A *partnership in learning* could be a useful description for the relationship between adults and children, teachers and learners in the twenty-first century school. It certainly moves the position along the spectrum from the power-coercion model so often the mechanism in many twentieth century schools. The second aspect worthy of analysis is around Deep Leadership and Organization and Design. Andy Hargreaves (1991) suggested that 'collegiality (was) rapidly becoming one of the new orthodoxies of educational change and school improvement' and yet the use of the term seems inappropriately applied. Hargreaves really refers to collaboration rather than the more advanced and richer concept of collegiality. Collaboration is certainly a strong feature of Government policy in the early years of the twenty-first century predicated on the principles of learning from each other, sharing effective practice and providing collective support. This is rather different from the prevailing climate of competition fostered in the 1990s through 'league tables' and target setting for school improvement. While these remain there is a dawning realization that continuous improvement is likely to be incremental, achieved through collaborative practice, for example, federations rather than competitive mutual destruction!

Team work within school management structures is an essential part of departmental / subject / faculty success. Working together, that is, collaborating on improvement, aspects of teaching and learning, methods of assessment and so on would be recognized in all schools. However the twin notions of teacher autonomy and teacher empowerment are extremely variable from school to school and it is here that leadership of twenty-first century schools needs to fundamentally reconsider both the philosophy and practice of leadership.

Andy Hargreaves (1992) talks about teacher culture and the different forms that emerge. The individualistic culture is identified by teachers working in isolation from one another; the Balkanized culture identifies power orientated, status emphasized groups who act in a competitive way. This group can be collaborative but in a way that emphasizes loyalty to the team/department not necessarily the whole. Andy Hargreaves (1992) perceives collaborative cultures to be very different exhibiting openness, trust and support within and beyond the team. The product of this culture moves beyond the classroom and school 'blurring the boundaries between in-school, out of school and . . . professional and personal . . . teachers work is deeply embedded in teachers lives' (p. 233).

The fourth culture is that of contrived collegiality that 'reconstitutes teacher relations in the administrators own image – regulating and reconstructing teachers' lives so that they support the predictable implementation of administrative plans and purposes, rather than creating the unpredictable development of teachers' own' (p. 234). Finally Hargreaves describes the 'moving mosaic' in which a coherent sense of purpose moves between the other cultures seeking a paradigm that creates an improved future.

Leadership in schools would recognize these types of teacher culture as present in all forms. School leaders tend to lean towards minimization of specific individualistic cultures but inevitably fluctuate around the other four. Hargreaves, in our view, fails to address true collegiality as a potential culture partly because in the time context of his research there was little evidence of such a thing but also the nature of school in relationship to curriculum, teacher professionalism and Government influence made true collegiality a non-starter.

There are significant barriers to collegiality. In the first place the organizational leader would need to surrender a significant degree of power; Heads of Department would likewise relinquish their *right of veto* and self/department determination. Teachers, and indeed all staff working within the school, would expect to have equal value, equal input and involvement in decision making and taking. The other side of this particular coin is the absolute requirement for mutual support, behaviours that value others as equals and a high degree of respect and trust. In all areas of professional activity, not simply teaching, there are variable human characteristics and traits that lead to a wide disparity of behaviour and attitude. Remuneration and promotion are also important parameters. In a truly collegiate structure should everyone be paid the same and would rank/status/position become an irrelevance? If this were the case where is the promotional pathway (referred to in Chapter 3) or is that a contradiction in terms?

As with all professional activity 'time in the job', experience, level of training, level of qualification impact on the quality of the person. For the sake of clarity it is possibly sensible to avoid the analysis that suggests that two people experiencing an identical input, for example, training course will come away with different interpretations that lead to one being better educated than the other! It is the nature of human beings that experiences will have different impacts and effects on every individual. One of the strengths of collegiate activity is that every participant is different.

Ritchie and Deakin-Crick (2007) argue that 'leadership' needs reconceptualizing moving from the traditional head of the organization towards an inclusive model in which all staff are involved in the process and practice of leadership. They acknowledge that it (leadership) 'is . . . a complex concept and that building leadership capacity through distributed leadership is no easy option' (p. 37). The size and context for this assertion is not localized or parochial, it has a global texture with most *communities* reaching a consensus.

Haycock (2007) provides a summative view where she says,

> When you meet the leaders in the places that are really getting the job done, they are not the kind of leaders that just turn things round by the sheer force of their personality. They are regular people, they are totally focussed. They are totally relentless. They are not big, outsized personalities and they are not the only leaders of their schools. Especially in the larger schools, the Principals know that they can't get it all done themselves. Those are the places that improve. Leadership is not about one person, it's about building a shared commitment and a shared team. (p. 2)

There is common agreement about the constituent parts of effective school leadership. At a base level, setting directions, developing people and redesigning the organization are common features. However, this remains a diverse concept with multiple perspectives that do not fully connect with collegiality. The leadership styles defined by Hay McBer (1998), used in the post National Professional Qualification for Headship (NPQH) development of established Headteachers in the UK Leadership Programme for Serving Heads (LPSH) sought to identify the predominant style of leadership in a given case. The range of styles from authoritative, coercive, democratic, pacesetting, affiliative to coaching often identified a particular Headteacher's preferred leadership style and thereby gave a clear insight into the type of school culture that was likely to emerge. Awareness of style led to personal, professional development towards the preferred style of outstanding leaders which was, unsurprisingly, a blend of all six! Ritchie and Crick (ibid.), citing the work of Harris (2004) consider distributed leadership and invitational leadership rather than imposed. Harris identifies distribution of responsibility, working through teams and collective responsibility as critical components. It is a central position in this chapter that distributed leadership is almost a half way house between authoritarian leadership and true collegiality. Extending the boundaries of leadership, challenging traditional hierarchies, creating a holistic blend of staff strengths and enthusiasms, collaborative purposeful action, leadership by different people at different times with a culture emphasizing autonomy and interdependence with effective internal accountability is an excellent description by Ritchie and Crick (p. 42) of distributed leadership and yet it seems to be insufficient for leadership in the twenty-first century.

At the heart of all debate on schools in the twenty-first century around learning, leadership and culture, is the learner. Discussions about leadership are, by their nature, in danger of maintaining an overarching 'doing it to' rather than 'doing it with'. Hopkins (2005), in leading a Think Tank for the National College for Schools Leadership (NCSL), developed ten propositions for school leadership:

1. School leadership must be purposeful, inclusive and values driven.
2. School leadership must embrace the distinction and inclusive context of the school.
3. School leadership must promote an active view of learning.
4. School leadership must be instructionally focused.

5. School leadership is a function that needs to be distributed through the school community.
6. School leadership must build capacity by developing the school as a learning community.
7. School leadership must be futures orientated and strategically driven.
8. School leadership must be developed through experimental and innovative methodologies.
9. School leadership must be served by a support and policy context that is systemic and implementation driven.
10. School leadership must be supported by an agency such as a National College that leads the discourse around leadership for learning.

The centrality of learning to these propositions quite correctly focuses the purposes of leadership towards improving the educational experience in schools. Hopkins derives the concept of instructional leadership which promotes student learning and engages parents as well as students as active participants in the process of learning. In Hopkins view instructional leadership consists of:

- Defining the values and purposes of the school (proposition 1)
- Managing the programme of teaching and curriculum (proposition 3 and 4) and
- Establishing the school as a professional learning community (proposition 6) (p. 2)

Instructional leaders are, therefore, expert in the design, management and monitoring of the instructional process and are adept in the organizational, strategic, instructional, personal and interpersonal domains. There is a clear recognition of the importance of a leader as an intelligent, skilful professional able to work effectively with and through people to achieve improved outcomes for all participants. By its nature instructional leadership is inclusive, collaborative and participative but still suggests that equality among professionals is not reflected in the organizational structure. More importantly it fails to fully engage the learner in the organizational structure beyond being the recipient or customer/client position. In terms of collegiality this definition of leadership still remains at the half-way house leaving school leadership and management further forward but not in a position to fully address the needs of learners in the twenty-first century. It alludes to, but does not address, the issues of student voice, democratic involvement of all members of the school community or education in the wider context. There is a sense that collaborative/participative leadership continues to look inwards reaffirming the self-managing school as primarily a self-interested entity. This is most certainly not a criticism but a question. Have the concepts of leadership being extrapolated far enough to radically refocus schools and education on the future? Time is not on our side and marginal or incremental steps to change may be insufficient in the context of a rapidly changing world.

In the late 1980s Caldwell and Spinks (1988) defined the self-managing school as one in a decentralized system being given a significant amount of authority and responsibility for its own decisions related to resource allocation and related matters. At the time this represented a radical step forward and was embraced in the UK, New Zealand, parts of Australia, Canada and the USA. Caldwell and Spinks (1998) followed this seminal work with *Beyond the Self Managing School* which portrayed a vision for schooling in the knowledge society. This gestalt took another radical step forward, calling for dramatic change in approaches to teaching and learning and a connectedness in curriculum. Schools as work places would be transformed in all aspects, eradicating practices associated with schools in the industrial age. The fabric of schools would need to change to facilitate the new approach to learning, embracing anytime-anyplace learning, global learning networks – schools, in the future, may be very different both conceptually and visibly. The gestalt elevated the role of the teacher as the processes of teaching and learning also undertook a paradigm shift (Professionalism and Great Teaching) envisioning teachers as a global collection sharing and working with each other. Caldwell and Spinks emphasized the capacity to work in teams and central to the transformation of schooling and recognized that, for the vision to become reality, subject boundaries would be broken, learning would become integrated across the curriculum, rigidity in the curriculum would be challenged as would those in roles, relationships and school organization. There is a coincident point here between the concept of instructional leadership and this vision of schools. However, it is more of a glancing blow than an absorption of the philosophy of the future school. In these schools teachers would have multiple, flexible roles, working within different teams as the occasion demanded; the experience would be raised, uplifting and above all of real value to the professional and the profession and to society.

The St John's curriculum is an example of how a school has moved towards realizing the vision created by Caldwell and Spinks. The concept of radical transformation is no longer an alien suggestion but one which many educators and business leaders worldwide would recognize and accept. There is still fear within the system which acts to constrain individuals and groups, fear of going too far or the fear of 'getting it wrong' or of public or political disdain. The central tenet of this book, and specifically this chapter, is that a new paradigm of leadership is required if the gestalt is to be fully realized. It is beyond current practice and at a point where many would fear to go. The challenge is, in part, to create school systems and schools that realize outstanding outcomes for all. To achieve this, a new professionalism must emerge. Networks and federations of schools have the potential to achieve this but are likely to be held back if the fundamentals of collegiality are not addressed. Participation in leadership is not sufficient nor is collaboration. Zuboff and Maxmin (2004) suggest that independence, self control and self-definition (in their terms *sanctuary and voice*) create interdependencies or *connection*. Caldwell (2004) describes this in the context of the self-managing school as 'engagement in a quest for connection'. In his description of the elements of the self-managing school Caldwell (ibid.) identifies the student as 'the most important unit of organisation – not the classroom, not the school and not the school system', and goes on to identify networks of schools with leadership distributed across schools, as well as within schools, as a preferred future to bring about transformation. It is our view that this will happen if the underlying principles are right but that real and radical transformation will be negated through conservatism and fear.

So how can collegiality overcome these obstacles? Fielding (1999) draws an interesting set of strands together for a redefined professionalism in education. The first strand is that at the centre of collegiality in education teachers seek opportunities, and are inclined to learn with and from each other. The second of the strands suggests that teaching is a personal activity and that 'at the heart of the educative encounter there is a mutuality of learning between the teacher and the student' (p. 21). Fielding identifies this as the point at which students enter the collegium, as partners in the learning process and not focal points of professional activity. Teachers are sometimes learners, students are sometimes teachers, not always cast in the role of perpetual learner. The final strand is a view that education is not the sole province of what goes on in the classroom or school but involves parents and the community. This effectively extends the collegium to those often disenfranchised. It is important to raise a distinction here between community/parental involvement (i.e. collaboration) and being part of the collegium. The latter is far deeper than the former.

The development of equality as a prerequisite to true collegiality though peer learning demands of collegiality that 'it transcends the instrumentalism and short-termism of activities and undertakings which bring teachers together within the rubric of an invasive managerialism or a merely prudential impulse' (Fielding ibid.: p. 21). This is in reality a re-professionalization of teaching but also recognition of professional equality within the collegium. Seeing students as agents of transformation, the implicit and explicit reciprocity between teachers and students emphasizes the authenticity of the learning. Listening to each other is a powerful position for learning. Co-creating the curriculum experience and the conditions for learning deepens the learning experience and also deepens the sense of mutual respect and understanding. A common theme in Nurturing Independent Thinkers (Bosher & Hazlewood 2005) was that learning and teaching are most exciting, most profound when the interface between learning and teaching are blurred and at times indistinguishable.

We entirely concur with Fielding when he states that

> talk of delivering the curriculum is disgusting and dishonest: disgusting because it replaces the ethically and experientially nuanced language of learning with the monologic, the mechanistic and the myopic; dishonest because learning cannot be sensibly conceived of in this way and therefore cannot be accomplished in this way either. (p. 23)

Openness and attentiveness to each other are fundamental to an engaged and productive learning experience. The natural consequence of this is that students deepen and develop their role in the learning context. At St John's this has become known as *Learning Walks* in which students are trained in research methodology and then become active participants in researching and analysing teaching practice sharing their findings with peers, teachers, parents and Governors. Fielding defines this as *radical collegiality* and explores the power of this approach to redefine and transform the processes of learning. The impact on structure and culture of the school is considerable. If transformation occurs at this level then the way in which the school as an organization is led and managed must also transform. The new professionalism that emerges through radical collegiality embraces the community dimension as partners in the collegium. It does not imply that the community somehow take an equal place in the professional collegium but that their voice and contribution informs the action of an enhanced professional structure. The dispositions, cultures and structures at the heart of radical collegiality create opportunities for reflection, discourse and action which raise the future game. 'Radical collegiality, thus becomes the dynamic of the dialogic school, a school whose boundaries and practices are not the prisoner of place and time, but rather the agent of increasingly inclusive community' (Fielding ibid.: p. 29).

The interface between Caldwell's vision and collegiality is now clear but the key question remains, how does a school leader implement collegiality? It is helpful to consider the position taken by Tasmanian Principals (TPA 2004). The proposals for leadership development identified five propositions:

1. Leadership starts from within
Effective educational leaders know themselves, act based on a well-formed set of values, have a high degree of self-efficacy and deep sense of commitment and responsibility. They have a clear personal vision for optimizing student learning and wellbeing and the courage and determination to achieve that vision.

2. Leadership is about influencing others
Effective educational leaders understand the nature of power and change and know the quality of the relationships they have with students, staff and the school community is crucial to their ability to influence and achieve desired outcomes.

3. Leadership develops a rich learning environment
Effective educational leaders know what supports and enhances teaching and learning, and how fundamental collaborative work and professional learning are to professional and organizational improvement and growth. They understand children and young people and their educational and social needs, are able to work expertly with teachers to ensure quality curriculum and support services, and are vigilant about student wellbeing and success.

4. Leadership builds professionalism and management capability
Effective educational leaders know that it is their responsibility to promote and support excellence in teaching and learning, and to be an advocate for professionalism in the community to maximize the value of the influential and important work that schools do.

5. Leadership inspires leadership actions and aspirations in others
Effective educational leaders know that they have a responsibility to promote and support widespread and sustainable leadership throughout the school, inspiring others to share this leadership so that learning and wellbeing are optimized.

(APAPDC Learn: Lead: Succeed 2004)

In 2006 St John's continued a process of management evolution that it had in effect begun in 2001 with the launch of the Alternative Curriculum (Bosher & Hazlewood ibid.). The curriculum was an integrated, theme based approach taught by a small inter-disciplinary group of teachers who planned, developed and learnt together. The approach engaged students as full partners in the learning process and became the forerunner of a collegiate approach. Over time the practice and curriculum deepened. As an integrated team there was no leader as such – simply highly committed professionals creating a rich learning experience.

The next two chapters capture the process of extending this approach to the whole school and embedding the language. It was and is however a difficult and complex process. In his book entitled *Change Matters*, Scott (1999) discusses the three insights which underpin change. The first of these *'Change is learning and learning is change'*, identifies that the doing of something new is in effect a learning process. The important driver and therefore motivator must be that those engaged in bringing about the change see it as relevant and useful both personally and to the organization. The second insight concerns the difference between *change* and *progress* where one is not necessarily the same as the other. For the two to have synchronicity the change must be in a desirable direction. This in turn is a matter of personal interpretation with respect to those involved in the change. The third insight describes the position that individual and organizational learning are inextricably linked. Scott makes the point clearly that not only must individuals be willingly committed to the change but must be enabled to bring it about effectively. Adaptation to the change by the individuals collectively ensures that the organization learns and accommodates the change.

In the context of collegiality and its close connection to improvements in the learning environment and pedagogical dynamic it stands to reason that improvement will involve change; sustaining the improvement will require infrastructure change to support this. The complexity of change means that successful change is very often a team effort in which the team learn together. This learning will involve learning from each other, coaching, mutual support and a commonly held belief that the change will be for the better. Change needs to be led but the important interconnection with collegiality is that collegiality recognizes that anyone can lead at a given time and the leader will emerge from consensus and negotiation by the team. This however presupposes that the past experience of the team both recognizes how this works and that it has the necessary permissions and authority to proceed.

In the educational context of our time, which will be explored more fully in Chapter 7, change is inevitable. The external forces impacting on society and education demand fast and far reaching change but are we equipped for this and can we move fast enough?

Reflecting on the five propositions for leadership there is a high degree of congruence between collegiality and leadership. In bringing about propositions 3–5 teamwork, collective understanding and commitment and united professionalism are all 'givens'. It is in the essence of 'leadership starts from within' that the secret lies. Truly effective leaders do not need to demand, instruct or use force. The highly evolved personal vision centred on strong values, deep commitment and personal empathy with others but focused on high aspirations, high ideals and the individuals in the organizations, enables such leaders to create an environment in which everyone feels of equal value, equal importance and has an equal contribution. This leads naturally to proposition two and hence to a logic which says, 'collegiality can work!'

As the Year 7 and 8 programmes moved to Year 9 the statutory requirements of Key Stage 3 SATs and GCSE courses effectively blocked further development, reverting to linear, non-integrated GCSE courses. The old divisions under subject leaders re-emerged and was possibly best described as sound collaborative practice against a backdrop of individual classrooms.

5 The 'management' of leadership

This chapter will be treated as more of a conversation, raising questions and suggesting solutions.

The leader of the leaders

Who leads the leaders? This is the title of the book and an interesting question to pose. Do the leaders need leading and /or managing is another question one might ask. This chapter will explore a number of questions but not necessarily provide all the answers. The right response to the questions for any organization is dependent on an infinite set of variables associated with the characteristics of that individual organization and the multiplicity of personality traits of the leaders in that organization. What is right for one may be totally inappropriate for another. This sounds like an interesting conundrum to resolve, but resolution is possible if undertaken in a systematic manner with a clear set of given parameters, guidelines or templates within which the solution must fall.

Let us start at the top of the organization with the leader. It is normally accepted by the members of an organization that those 'at the top' and particularly the one right at the top, in whatever context you wish to interpret that term, is the one setting the pace. This is the individual and the Strategic Leadership Team is the group to which all other members of the organization will turn for executive decisions, direction and tone which will then permeate throughout the organization. It is important to recognize that throughout history, some leadership has been found wanting. Andrew Law, Canadian Prime Minister 1858–1923 made the interesting statement, 'I must follow them; I am their leader' (Rees 1999: p. 345). This is an interesting repeat of the words of the French Minister of the Interior Alexandre Ledru-Rollin 1848 during the French Revolution, when he felt bound to follow the mob rather than make a principled stand, followed at a later date by Churchill's parody of the quotation in a criticism of Clement Atlee's leadership of the country as Prime Minister. It is important that the leader stands for all the ideals of the organization, and leads from the front, not be frightened by consequences or opposition when the going gets tough. However, the leader must also have the organization's direction and vision to the forefront of all intention and action lest the organization falls into the situation highlighted in St Matthew's Gospel 15.14: 'They be blind leaders of the blind. And if the blind lead the blind, both shall fall into the ditch' (Rees 1999: p. 101).

There is little to be gained by blithely ploughing forwards if direction and purpose are unclear. Jack Welch, the former chairman and CEO of General Electric Co. said, 'good business leaders create a vision, articulate the vision, passionately own the vision and relentlessly drive it towards completion' (Hakala 2008). It is imperative that the person at the top drives the organization forwards. Who leads this leader is unanswerable. It clearly depends on the individual and the group to which this leader is attached. For the most part, the leadership of the person at the pinnacle of the organization leads by dint of his or her own personality. He or she will have most of the personality traits listed below in some sort of combination together with high levels of self-esteem and self-confidence. This personality profile is often mediated by internal and external forces that are brought to bear. Such forces, as market position, expected performance of the individual and the company, associated stakeholders, clients, Government statute and dictated direction and internal performance criteria.

Research shows that for smaller organizations, the origin of the organization is often from a single individual. They had the initial idea, the money to make it work and the initial vision to take the idea forwards. From this small start the organization expands, taking more employees on with this expansion. In this scenario, it is the leader at the top who leads. As the organization continues to increase in size and complexity, so the leading becomes more diversified. It is at this point that guidance with leading the leaders is often necessary. Even in small organizations, it does not necessarily need to be a 'one man band'.

There is a dichotomy developing here. It has long been considered in management and leadership circles that it is the leader who provides the strength to the organization, and indeed that is so. However let us consider what makes a good organization stronger. Chapter 4 showed that strong direction and decisive decision making can be very effectively achieved by leadership and management by groups as well as an individual if they work in a collegiate manner, and even stronger if the concept of radical collegiality is in operation. In the last century, Her Majesty's Inspectorate (HMI) had the opinion that good schools could only be achieved solely by the strong leadership of the Headteacher. In their influential publication *Matters for Discussion* series (DES 1977: p. 36) they quoted information from '*10 Good Schools*' in the first paper and made the observation about the ten good schools chosen: 'What they all have in common is effective leadership and a "climate" that is conducive to growth . . . Emphasis is laid on consultation, teamwork and participation, but without exception, the most important single factor in the success of these schools is the quality of leadership of the head.'

This is an interesting viewpoint because it separates the process of participative decision-making and the concept of working in teams from the characteristic traits of the head leader. Decision making and taking is a process that can be shared, and from the evidence in Chapter 4, the case history shows just how successfully. Collegiality gets away from the often-quoted concept of leadership as a series of personal qualities held only by the leader. Hakala (2008) identified the following leadership traits.

- Excellent communication skills to be able to communicate the organization's vision in terms that members of the organization are convinced by. He rightly states that 'passion is contagious'.
- Disciplined to work towards the vision single-handed as well as encouraging the members of the organization to contribute towards it.
- Integrity to combine the outer actions of the organization with its inner values, both as a corporate body and as an individual. Combined with this is the characteristic of honesty.
- Dedication to complete the task. Leaders inspire dedication by example. 'Leaders show that there are no nine-to-five jobs, only opportunities to achieve something great.'
- Magnanimity to give credit where credit is due. As part of this attribute, 'a leader takes personal responsibility for failure. This sort of reverse magnanimity helps other people to feel good about themselves and draws people together'. In order to do this, it is important that leaders have a sense of humility. These types of leaders can then recognize that they are no better or worse than other members of the team, and they are 'happy to spread the fame and take the blame'.
- Openness in leaders means that they are willing to listen to others ideas, and they are able to 'suspend judgement whilst listening to others ideas as well as accept new ways of doing things that someone else thought of'.

- Creativity, the ability to think differently.
- Fairness, the act of dealing with others consistently and justly.
- Assertiveness, all leaders must be this in order to get things done without any misunderstanding of what is required.
- A sense of humour to relieve tension, prevent boredom and defuse hostility.

Added to these traits, two more should be considered for inclusion. The traits of courage and risk taking are often mentioned as being possessed by good leaders, and Chris Satterthwaite of Chime Communications, James Barkhouse of Syngenta and Patrick Hazlewood of St John's School all felt that they possessed these traits and that they very important facets of their personal leadership success.

It is true that without a strong leader who exhibits many of the characteristics identified with good leadership the organization will flounder. However, these characteristics are not necessarily just the leader's domain. It could be argued that many individuals in a team who are part of a collegial approach could also exhibit and use those same leadership traits to the group advantage of that team. The strength of the organization lies with the leader who recognizes this and harnesses the power that ensues from such a wealth of talent. It is then that the traits of integrity, humility, magnanimity and fairness become a required strength for the leader at the top.

One's thoughts might turn, as a comparison, to the fabled autocratic ownership of mines and mills during the English Industrial Revolution. The stereotypical view of these men, they were all men because emancipation had not occurred during this period, was that of a single owner not willing to share views, wealth or success with anyone. The owner's decision was the only decision, and that decision was final and non-negotiable. This entrenched position, as the history books show, led to inflexibility, an inability to adapt and move with the times and eventually closure through lack of competitiveness.

In answer to the first question in this chapter about who leads the leader, it is impossible to pinpoint a specific person or event. What is clear, is that the leader at the top must possess a number of significant personality traits, be a team player and be responsive to pressures internally and externally if he or she is to lead effectively. He or she may take advice on direction and focus, but I suspect in the end, the natural leaders' flair, gut instinct and wide appreciation of the big picture are the things that will guide his or her decision making.

Managing the other leaders in the organization

Having clarified the position of the leader at the top, the next task is to address those in leadership positions at other and different levels in an organization. The second question of do leaders need leading is definitely 'yes'. Not only do they need leading, they also need managing. This is not because they lack the prerequisite skills to undertake leadership. But because there needs to be a sense of coordinated thought and action across the organization which is both sympathetic to the aims of that organization, and accommodating enough to autonomous action and informed decision making and taking to take place inside a collegiate envelope.

In many ways, this concept of 'managing' the leadership process is at the heart of the book. Leadership and management go hand in hand in any organization regardless of size. The difference is that the larger and the more complex the organization, the more potential layers of management there are and therefore the more layers of leadership managing activity needs to be in place to accommodate the complexity. Leadership is an active process requiring vision, charisma, logical application and a confident approach to solutions or situations, and in order to achieve the desired end point, it has to have active input and constant directional readjustment to pull the direction into line.

Can leaders be developed or are they born? . . . a debate that has raged for years. This is not an easy question to answer, but if pushed for a definitive response, it is probable that leaders are born. When one looks back at world leaders, such as Winston Churchill, Mahatma Gandhi, Nelson Mandela, Mother Theresa, Otto Bismarck, U Thant, and perhaps surprisingly Ronald Regan and his creation of a better understanding between Margaret Thatcher and himself representing the western world, and the USSR in the 1980s, all of these individuals have that extra personality factor not found in the majority of the population. What is it that makes these individuals stand out from the crowd? Perhaps it is captured in the thoughts of Smith (1996: p. 30) who defined leadership as:

> A quality that makes people listen to them. Potential leaders have a 'holding court' quality about them. When they speak, people listen. Other people may talk a great deal, but nobody listens to them. They're making a speech; they're not giving leadership. I take notice of people to whom others listen.

These are exceptional people, with finely developed attributes and skills, but with an extra dimension. They were in the right place at the right time to use those given skills to the best advantage. On occasions it was a country or an individual in crisis that brought those skills to the forefront. One could argue that anyone could have taken the lead in these moments of trouble, but it is significant that it was these people out of millions who took up the position at the front and took the rest of the people with them.

For mere mortals, the second part to the question of whether leaders are born or can be created is an appreciation that there is room for the development of leaders and leadership potential. Many if not most organizations have many 'leaders' within their midst and without a doubt, leadership qualities can be developed and encouraged. Many hours of research have been spent and professional development courses developed to encourage individuals to hone their skills in leadership.

Organizations like Her Majesty's Armed Forces have very appropriate tools both to recognize and develop leadership potential, and they use it to great effect in the appointment of officers to lead service personnel. Not all of these individuals possess that special spark of the exceptional leader, but all selected are able to lead others and set the example required for their organization. The raw material of leadership has to be part of them, and what any system must then do is bring those qualities to the fore, develop and hone them and give the individual both the confidence to use those traits, and provide the environment in which those leadership skills and traits will be used most effectively.

Creating leaders

In most groups of people, there are those who are happy to follow, sometimes blindly, and others who wish to, and have the skills to lead. This natural asset to lead needs recognizing, honing and developing before that individual is able to play an effective role in the organization. The National College for School Leadership's *Fast Track* programme for developing teachers into leaders and managers in a short period of time is an example of continuing professional development that is open to the teaching profession. There is no substitute for experience of the job on the ground. A theoretical and academic background to leadership is a necessary adjunct, but getting experience of the job on the 'shop floor' is the real guide to what is required for management. The wise head of the organization is constantly trawling through the workforce looking for potential leaders for the future, and giving them development opportunities on which to 'cut their leadership teeth'. Additionally, the head leader should be looking at vacancies as and when they occur in the organization to bring new and fresh members to the leadership team/s that have accumulated skills and experience elsewhere. Effective teams have to be created and designed; they do not happen by chance. The position is not as simplistic as this however, as any team in any organization is a dynamic entity. Some people blossom given leadership opportunities and responsibilities; others reach their full and potential ceiling very quickly and are unable to develop further. This situation needs careful handling. This type of person is identified by regular and rigorous performance management processes, and then needs appropriate professional development in an attempt to take them forwards or to divert them into other activities in the organization where their skills and experience can still make a useful contribution.

The head leader needs a degree of ruthlessness, single mindedness and a strong conviction in what he or she is doing to bring an effective leadership team to fruition. The process of selection is crucial, with the first task being an identification of job role, skills required and personal attributes required to complement the existing team members. When these are clearly established, it is then time to appoint personnel to fulfil those roles. The danger and temptation in many organizations undergoing change or development is to make the existing personnel fit roles to which they are not suited or do not have the skills to fulfil. This is a built in disaster scenario. The head leader needs to be firm, positive and brave in selection; the team that he or she wants will then develop.

Creating leadership teams

Before exploring the management of leadership in detail, it is a priority for the organization to satisfy itself that it has an experienced, effective and supportive strategic leadership team who understand and are able to manage the leaders under their control. Having posited the idea that exemplary leaders are born, any organization would be foolish not to recognize that its leadership teams can contain good strong leaders who can be developed over time given the appropriate levels of experience, exposure to risk and the security of accountable decision making.

Let us explore these ideas in more detail. Strong effective and thriving organizations are only so because of the strong leadership at the top supported by an effective strategic leadership team. To develop such a team, the organization must have the following culture and ethos in place, as detailed in Figure 5.1.

So how does an organization develop such a team? As mentioned in a previous chapter, it is perhaps helpful to have Belbin's Team Role Inventory (West 1994) in the back of the organization's mind. The nine team types make for an effective balance. These teams are based on research of 200 teams from a variety of business, commerce and education organizations undertaken by the Administrative Staff College at Henley in the UK. Many teams may not be large enough to contain one of each of the roles shown in Figure 5.2, nor may the organization set out to fill a leadership team exclusively comprised on one of each of these roles. The reality of most leadership teams is that there will be a number of these role members present, and some of the team may be

Culture	Ethos
Vision oriented	Understanding
Willingness to embrace change	Humility
Desire to do the best for the organization	Empathy
Enjoy and celebrate success	Self-confidence
Recognize failure and look for positive remedial action	Recognized expertise
Prepared to multitask	Earned respect from the workforce
Prepared to share work load	People oriented
Able to delegate authority not abdicate responsibilities	Team member
Understand accountability and embrace it as a positive process	Appropriate channels of communication
Considered and calculated risk taking	Hard work and dedication
Freedom for controlled experimentation	Loyalty to the organization
Prepared to assume temporary or permanent responsibility with confidence	Loyalty to the head of the organization

Figure 5.1 Cultural and ethos requirements for successful leadership teams

Coordinator	Resource Investigator	Team Worker
Shaper	Company Worker / Implementer	Completer / Finisher
Plant	Monitor / Evaluator	Specialist

Figure 5.2 Belbin's team roles (West 1994)

able to fulfil a number of the roles. It is just a guide, based on research that shows that leadership teams containing these types of people tend to be successful high achieving teams.

Just having teams containing these roles is not sufficient to guarantee success. The right cultural environment is crucial to complement these skills. Figure 5.2 shows the culture that must be in place. The development of the right culture was discussed in Chapter 2, and this is almost always unique to the organization. Members of the leadership team must be experienced, feel free, confident and empowered to take and make decisions without fear of retribution. They must share the vision and goals of the head leader and understand how the direction of the organization is going to achieve those goals and aims. The team must also exist in an encouraging forward looking 'on the edge' environment with success forever being just out of grasp. James Barkhouse of Syngenta leads his team in just that 'on the edge' environment, never totally satisfied with the performance of the present and always looking forwards to improved performance in the future. This takes dynamic teams forward at pace and does not allow for the 'plateauing effect' (Bosher & Hazlewood 2005) to occur.

With a confident leader in place, surrounded by an experienced, motivated and forward looking leadership team, the process of managing the leaders can now be approached.

A tool box of leadership approaches and strategies

The subliminal management process

What do we mean by this form of leadership/management approach? Ann Jones (1987: p. 10) makes the opening stance for this part of the managing leadership process.

She says:

> Giving other people genuine authority does not mean giving up one's own authority; empowering others does not mean enfeebling oneself; encouraging others to give creative leadership does not mean abdicating from having ideas of one's own; giving others real responsibility does not mean leaving them to sink or swim, but rather to support them in developing the best possible way of going forward.

The rules are simple; an effective and dynamic senior or strategic leadership team have clear responsibilities for themselves, their colleagues and to the organization itself. Jones (1987) has the balance right in indicating that there has to be give and take in the process of the management and leadership, and that support always has to be in place. Staff have to feel that they are not on their own, particularly when making difficult unpleasant or unpopular decisions. They should be trained, encouraged and allowed to experience difficult decision making. If the culture is right, even if mistakes are made, they must feel supported by those considered by the organization's members to be at the top. Members of the organization have to feel and be involved in the process of the organization's operations. At the same time, the leaders have to be directing operations in some form or other, either overtly or covertly. While there is no suggestion here of hidden or underhand methodologies, there is certainly a managerial strategy to be employed in 'managing' which brings about the required outcomes.

The talk so far has led the reader towards still thinking in conventional terms about a hierarchical structure to the organization. Chapter 4 showed that it is possible to move away from this type of leadership model. While every organization has to have a stated and recognized leader at the head for legal reasons, collegiality within the organization means that essentially there is no one at the top, because there is not a top; only a series of groups or teams working in a coordinated way towards a common end.

It does not matter what sort of leadership structure is in place, there is a strategic benefit to the concept of subliminal managing. The art of suggestion and quiet repetition is a sensitive strategy to undertake. It often happens by accident, but many bold leaders clearly undertake the process with considered intent. It happens in a considered way by the lead leader having made a decision in his or her mind of the direction in which the next strategic move is to be made. The skill is to then manage all discussion, arguments and decisions in favour of that direction without actually stating it. It has already been said that the good leader must have excellent communication skills, and these are used to the full during this management strategy. Every opportunity is grasped by the lead leader to reinforce the favoured direction. The emphasis of key words on a chart; convincing arguments presented using a variety of media vehicles, surreptitious placing of documents or reading materials to which all have common access. Repetition of favoured words or phrase with emphasis on the key areas during discussions, summing up outcomes to leave the desired outcomes as a lasting impression are all strategies which can be used. Opportune timing can also be a useful tool. If the desired outcome is left as the final impression or bullet point of several options at the end of a meeting, argument, discussion or presentation it is the one idea that is carried away in the minds of the personnel who are at the meeting. All presenters know that a presentation should contain no more than three points in a summary of that presentation. It becomes very important that in subliminal management, the key points are the points that are left in the minds of the recipients.

This process may seem a little underhand, but it is a quite legitimate way of displaying possible alternative ideas and options, it just leaves an imprint in people's minds for the future. The central key of this strategy is that the final outcome is deemed by all concerned to have been reached by consensus and agreement, rather than a decision foisted on the workforce by 'the boss'.

The power of suggestion – sowing the seeds

An alternative strategy or maybe one to be used in conjunction with subliminal management is that of suggestion. During this strategy, the desired outcome is put forward convincingly by one or several members of the group. The power of good communication skills is a necessary prerequisite for this approach. Once again, there is a need for the leader, manager or proponent of the idea to have a clear view of the desired outcome and the most appropriate route to get to that outcome. Using this strategy, the leader or proponent is clearly visible as the one making the suggestion. He or she must put forward the most convincing argument in order to win the consent and agreement of the rest of the group. Not only must the argument be the most convincing, but the dialogue needs to be so powerful that alternative arguments and outcomes are seen as obviously inferior. Data, statistical evidence, current and previous research and case history are all legitimate tools to use in providing solidity for the argument. The presentation of these facts is stage one of the strategy. Stage two onwards is to continually and constantly re-rehearse the strong and convincing points in favour of the desired outcome as often as possible. The 'drip drip' effect is the strategy to be used. This is quite an overt process and makes no apologies for the persuasive powers of an articulate proposer. The manager of this strategy seizes every available opportunity to promote and re-visits the positive factors associated with the proposer's desired outcome. Eventually from experience, it becomes part of the groups' understanding and, to a point where cleverly, they the group feel that it is them who have had the idea. Once this acceptance has taken place, the desired decision is taken and all are in agreement.

The stalking horse approach

This is a different strategy altogether. Using this strategy, the leader, manager or proponent of an idea uses a third party either wittingly or unwittingly to bring about the desired outcome. The method behind this strategy is to propose or put into place an idea that masks or overshadows the true and desired outcome. The group consider this stalking horse idea without being aware that it has been placed there on purpose. The parents of teenage children will be very aware of this strategy employed by their children. How often have parents been involved in the following dialogue?

> Alison: *Dad, can I go to Lisa's party tonight and stay out until 04.00 a.m.?*
> Dad: *Certainly not, 04.00 a.m. is far too late for a girl of your age to be out even if it is a weekend.*
> Alison: *Can I stay just until midnight then?*
> Dad: *I am happy if you promise to be home by midnight.*

Unknown to the parent of course, the daughter clearly knew that permission would never be granted for a stay until 04.0 a.m., but also knew from previous experience that a midnight extension was a distinct possibility. A stalking horse of a highly improbable outcome had been used to achieve what was always going to be the desired outcome. In the same way, managerial and leadership outcomes can be achieved using the same techniques. Improbable positions, posts or suggestions are tabled as the way forwards with the hidden desired direction as a second but seemingly weaker suggestion. Once the group considers these controversial and sometimes outrageous suggestions and considers their validity and appropriateness, the compromise weaker suggestion becomes the default. A rueful smile might just cross the manager's visage at this point!

The desired outcome has again been achieved by using another strategy from the leadership tool box.

Keeping it quiet and letting it happen

There are occasions when to keep quiet as the leader is the best strategy. If the groundwork for the idea or the argument has been well prepared, the quiet approach is the best way forwards. This is decidedly a risk strategy that has to be used with care. In many groups there are outspoken, arrogant or on some occasions ill informed individuals who will do your arguing for you by their negative approach and their outrageous alternative suggestions. It must be stressed again that the desired outcome must already be on the table as a possible outcome with all the sound reasoning to support it. If you have the courage to do it, and can rely on the group's intuitive ability to select the most appropriate outcome, then give the outrageous their opportunity. Their presentation will bring out counter suggestions from the sensible floor of the discussion and as if by magic, the support for the desired suggestion will slowly turn. The voice of reason in its fight against the unreasonable suggestions will become the direction. What must be guarded against in this scenario is to engage in counter argument which will lead to an open 'shouting match' and the opportunity for success lost. Keep quiet, let the voice of reason and common sense speak the loudest against the voice of unreason. Once again, let the group do the arguing, sit back as the proponent of the sound idea and let others argue the case for you. It is a risky strategy, because the unreasonable may win the day, but if that occurs, it is because the preparatory work has not been undertaken carefully enough. If the unreasonable win the day, then a more overt challenge will be necessary if the desired outcome is to be achieved.

The subtle prod

Here is a more gentle approach to obtaining the desired outcome. Most groups come to their decisions as a result of discussion, augment and counter argument. All fuelled by data, hypotheses and case history. To use the 'subtle prod' technique, requires team work. The basis of this approach to reaching the required decision is to gently direct thoughts and discussion towards the required outcome. Working in at least a team of two, the approach is for the lead person to propound the concept together with the supporting arguments. The second person in the team actively supports the argument from behind. That is to say, quietly supports the facts presented in such a manner that the overall effect of the presentation is to slightly magnify the quality of the argument. If a group realize that two influential people in the group are supporting the proposal then those who are undecided soon become convinced and join the supporting group. In addition, the 'subtle prod' can be used by an individual with a specific aim in mind. What happens is that at the appropriate opportunities in discussions and conversations, the key supporting points for the desired outcome are brought into the conversations as a gentle reminder. The value and validity of the proposal are constantly rehearsed and re-rehearsed but in a quiet and subtle manner. It is part of the subliminal approach in keeping the desired outcome to the forefront of the group's mind. The ability for the leader to bring about this strategy is reinforced by the next strategy in the tool box.

The Trojan horse approach

This famous stratagem whereby the Greeks sent a party of men into Troy hidden in a hollow wooden horse was part of the cycle of Troy sagas known to Homer . . . Sinon [a Greek who pretends to be a deserter] persuades the Trojans that the Greeks have given up and sailed away for good, leaving behind the horse as an offering to Athene . . . Then Sinon lets the Greeks out at night, and the gates are opened to the main army.
Radice (1971)

This is a more covert management strategy. Chapter 1 referred to the use of the strategy in connection with the implementation of the Curriculum Schools concept. The strategy is a risky and subtle approach to change. It is implemented by introducing a concept that is known and understood by those involved in change, but with a hidden agenda clothed within it. To further explain this process, the Trojan horse in the case study of St John's was the concept of the division of the management of the staff into curriculum schools. This is a common procedure adopted by many schools. Hidden within this concept, the Headteacher had laid out the more contentious argument for the dissolution of subject titles and management by Heads of Department altogether but left the teams intact to undertake the collegiality processes outlined in Chapter 4. It is then left to the members of the teams involved to discover for themselves the real concept hidden in the arguments. If this risky strategy works, then it is very effective because once again all members of the team support the argument because it is they who have in essence devised it. The really subtle leader has embedded the concepts in such a way that they are discovered rather than resulted by overt direction by the head leader.

The art of prior lobbying the bright or right people – which strategy to choose?

There are two strands to this strategy. 'Lobbying' as a term has its history in the political activity and is defined in the *COD* (1999) as: *a group of people trying to influence legislators on a particular issue; an organised attempt by members of the public to influence legislators.* So in leadership activities, it is the art of prior convincing others in the group of the quality of your argument so as to enlist their support or their vote when it comes to decision making and taking. This is a well known and well tried process which occurs in many different areas. It is often carried out prior to the meeting of the group so that there is a body of agreement already in place before the issue is raised. The more of the group supporting the idea in the meeting or discussion, the more likely the desired outcome is of being achieved.

The decision of who to lobby is an interesting discussion. There are several options. One is to lobby the bright people in the group. This presupposes that this group will easily see the quality and sense of the arguments being put forward and add their voice in convincing the rest. An alternative approach is to lobby the members of the group who seem to be in two minds over the issue. Start the lobbying early, well before the meeting and rehearse the positive arguments that will be convincing, together with countering opposing arguments which leave the waivers with a positive view of the desired outcome. The third group that could be lobbied are the right people who carry the most respect or influence with the group. This requires the presenter of the idea to have a view of who these people are, and have sufficient standing with them to be convincing in the arguments being put forward. As far as the group is concerned, if the 'right' people are seen to be supporting the motion, it is often difficult for those with less standing to vote against the perceived wisdom. The right people can also be those in the group who carry the esteem of the group through their previous actions or experience. Often less experienced members of the group can and will be swayed by the arguments presented or supported by more experienced colleagues just because they are venerated as being older and wiser in the field under discussion.

The decision about who to lobby is left to the experience and cunning wiles of the idea presenter. Who to lobby may change according to the decision or outcome required, and the more experienced or wily the leader, the better he or she knows the group, and the more convincing the arguments in support of the decision are, will alter who is approached and how.

How to decide on the best approach to achieve the stated goal

This is a difficult decision to make, and almost impossible to be dogmatic and prescriptive about. Once again, it comes down to the abilities and experience of the leader. What is clear is that there are a number of strategies for 'winning the argument' in the tool box. The leader must select often from experience, but sometimes purely on 'gut instinct' which of these strategies will best suit the situation. It comes down again to leadership personality traits. The risk taker might be more inclined to undertake the more high risk strategies, the more conservative leader may wish to choose the more supportive and safer lobbying approach. It all depends on the question, the decision required and leadership abilities. What all leaders should have is the skill to undertake the various strategies, and the experience to have tried them before.

From this chapter, it is clear that leadership cannot and does not 'just happen'. If the right decisions are to be made, in the eyes of the head leader and the strategic leadership team, then that decision making process and the people that make them have to be managed. There is no set formula for how this is done, but it has to be done.

Getting the big wheel to turn – how to overcome the inertia of generations

6

This chapter starts with an imaginary story by Jane Spiro (2008). The story depicts a journey through a situation that draws parallels with the journey that any organization is likely to take in the creation, introduction, development and implementation phases of a new initiative. We would like your imagination to wander as the story unwinds, and see if you like us can see some parallels between the journey depicted in the story, and the journey undertaken by organizations on the journey of change. In the story, there is a realization of a journey to be undertaken, the barriers to be overcome and the discovery in the end that it is the individuals and the groups involved who will eventually make the difference and achieve the goal.

Eye and the fellow-traveller

One day I came to the edge of a cliff. I had not realised the journey would end so suddenly and dangerously; but there seemed no way forward, and the way back was blocked by a strange and faceless creature that stood with his huge arms stretched across my path.

'Only members of the Laurel Crown Club may proceed,' he said.

'Which Club is that?' I cried, tired from all my many travels, 'and how can I join it?'

'You join it by following my dance, step by step, and after each step, proving you are as good as I am.'

'But that's ridiculous,' I said. 'Why should I want to do that? Look, here is the garland of the storyteller, woven by myself from a thousand stories.'

'That is nothing,' said the creature.

'And here is the crown of the teacher, made of shells excavated from the shores of four continents and threaded together with spun learning.'

The faceless creature laughed a bitter icy laugh.

'None of these will bring you the Laurel Crown, because none of the steps are like mine,' he crowed. 'Without this, how do I know you have the strength to continue the journey?'

'Because of all the journeys I've already travelled!' I shouted. 'The bridge-building journey, the river-crossing, the boat-making, the flower-blooming, the story-making, the wisdom-excavating journeys. Do none of those count?'

'None are mine!' yelled the creature. 'And I, Thought Doctor, am the only one that can lead the way. Take my journey back or none at all.'

'OK, if you must, show me the way then. Since I have travelled so far, I might as well do this further journey.'

Thought Doctor pointed with his long bony finger towards the hills. I noticed a long narrow track like a railway that burned an unbending route through the valleys, tunnelled through the hillside, and plunged into the woods the other side.

'That's it,' he said. 'You follow me, along the track, copying my dance, and at the end you win the crown.'

The journey seemed possible, and better than throwing myself over the cliff. But still, it did not seem a very exciting or useful way to travel, with so much landscape to explore on either side of the narrow track, and so many ways to explore apart from following his single step. And how would I carry with me all the garlands, sarongs, shells, and songs of previous journeys, if I was not allowed to offer them and share them on the way?

I threw myself down onto the grassy ground to think about my options. As I did so, I noticed appearing from behind Thought Doctor's cloak, a silent group of people, cloaked, pale and downcast, gathering around me on the cliff.

'We are members of the Laurel Crown Club,' they said.

I looked at them now as they stood nearer me.

'But you all look the same!' I cried.

'When we started we were all different,' one of them said, 'but by the end we have all learnt Thought Doctor's moves so well, we look just like him.'

'If you are Laurel Crown members, where are your crowns?'

'Here!' said one, and threw off his hood to reveal a shiny metallic crown that looked far too heavy for him and made him stoop forward.

'Here!' said another and revealed the same metallic shiny crown but it was so large it kept dropping over her eyes, and she had to push it up every few minutes.

'Here!' said another, and there was the crown again, but every so often the poor owner picked up a corner and began scratching underneath, shifting it round so it would sit more comfortably.

'None of your crowns fit!' I cried, concerned for them.

They laughed in chorus, like a pond of hippopotami.

'Of course not. There's only one size crown. If it doesn't fit, well that's just too bad. They all need to be the same size, to make sure it's all fair.'

'But being just the same size makes it NOT fair,' I cried.

Thought Doctor rolled his eyes, exasperated, and turned away.

'She clearly doesn't understand,' he snorted. 'Come, Club, let's leave her here to think.'

I sat by the cliff edge, suddenly alone, and looked in both directions. In one direction was a sheer drop down to a fast running river gorge. On the other was the Laurel Crown track, long and straight, with bunches of flowers every so often along the route where travellers had failed to survive. What to do? Now, with the Thought Doctor gone, there seemed to be many more possibilities. Looking again at the landscape ahead, it seemed laughable that there should be only one track forwards; on the contrary, there seemed to be an infinite number of paths, and surely nothing would stop me exploring them?

Encouraged by this thought, I stood up and again reviewed my options. In one direction was open hillside scattered with a blue dusting of heather; in the other direction was the path I had come from, winding over the cliff edge and dropping back down to a chain of rocky bays. I chose the new direction, the open hillside. Surely, if I set foot there, Thought Doctor wouldn't stop me?

So I began the new path, into the blue heather and the unmarked terrain. It was welcoming underfoot, and comforting to walk inland away from the cliff edge, wading through the tall grass, not knowing where it would lead me. After a while, as I walked, I suddenly became aware that there was a Fellow Traveller quietly beside me, and like me, quietly tracing the path of the wild flowers. I looked up to take note of him, and to my surprise, saw he was wearing a crown too.

'Oh! Your crown fits!' I cried.

'Of course it does,' said Fellow Traveller. 'I made it myself.'

We carried on walking, quietly for a while.

'But is it a Laurel Crown, like the others?'

'Yes, of course it is.'

'But did you do that long journey, like the others?'

'Yes, yes I did,' said the Traveller patiently.

'But how is it you don't look just like all the others? How is it you have strayed off the track?'

'Well I worked out the route for myself.'

'Is that allowed?'

'Of course it is. That's what I did, and I have a Crown and it fits just fine.'

I could see that all of those things were true. It seemed a much more interesting way to become a member of the Club.

'Could you show me how I might get a Crown that way too?'

'Sure, of course.'

We carried on walking, and the Fellow Traveller didn't seem to be showing me anything at all, but just following where I went along the hillside.

'But you aren't showing me. Shouldn't you be showing me the way?'

'No, quite the reverse. You choose which way you want to go, and I'll come along with you.'

'Are you sure?' I asked, nervously. It seemed a strange way to lead, to be in fact a follower.

'Look, the end of the journey is over there.' He pointed beyond the wood where the narrow track disappeared. 'You can get there any way you like.'

I took from my sack a handful of shiny stones gathered from a Mexican beach and threw them down.

'Can I use these as stepping stones?'

'Sure, of course,' and we jumped from one to the other, first me, and Fellow Traveller following.

'Take a stepping stone to put in your crown,' he said, as we reached the end. 'Now, where next?'

'If I scatter the marigold garland we could follow its scent.'

'Sure, try that,' said Fellow Traveller.

It was tiring, running after the scent of the marigold as it blew in the wind, and at the end, I threw myself down on a rock and sighed.

'I don't know where to go next.'

'Yes you do. Look in your bag.'

'I've nothing there. Nothing useful at all.'

'Of course you have. Tell me what's there.'

'A sari from India, a sarong from Hawaii, a branch from the learning tree, a . . .'

'OK, let's start with the first one. Find out where the sari wants us to go next.'

I took the sari out of its bag. It was buttercup yellow with streaks of quiet lavender, and as it unfolded from the bag it began to blow like a sail towards the east.

'There we are then,' said Fellow Traveller, 'that's the direction we have to go in.'

So we followed the sail of the sari, and then the kite of the sarong; and then the branch of the learning tree doused us around the Tors and I hardly knew we had travelled so far before I realised the station had appeared at the end of the Thought Doctor's narrow track.

'Do you mean we are nearly there?'

'Sure. You need to get your laurel crown ready for submission to the Club.'

'Oh no, one of those terrible metal ones that fall over your eyes and itch?'

Fellow Traveller laughed.

'A made-to-measure one, made with all the mementoes of your journey. It will take two months to craft.'

'Are you sure?' I said. 'Will it be as good as the others?'

'Well, I think it might be better, because for one thing it will fit, for another it will be quite unique and for another it will tell the story of your journey.'

In a quiet place at the station gates, I unfolded all the contents of my travels around me and spread them on the ground. How to fit them together? Surely they could never be crafted into one coherent and beautiful piece?

But as I stared at them hour after hour alone now outside the gates of my destination, it all became clear.

The learning branch was the centre of the crown. It had grown from a seed I had planted in childhood, and the roots had spread deeply and widely into the earth. After years of watering and nurturing, it had grown into a strong and fragrant tree with branches green with budding life. One of these branches became the anchor that held the crown together. Then I took the stepping stones I had gathered from the four continents and were shiny with all the times I had jumped from one to another, crossing streams and rivers and quick-sands and water-meadows, where they gave me strong and stable footing.

I bound these together on the anchor-branch, using the learning thread, the gold thread that bound and connected stories. The front of the crown was now secure.

Then I rolled the lavender and buttercup sari and the sarong with the silver fish and turtles, into long narrow drapes and plaited them together with the learning thread to hold the branch in place. They were the colours and textures I became on my journeys; they were the chameleon that blended with their worlds. The crown was now fragrant and colourful as a spring garden.

Then I lifted it to my head, and tied the plaited fronds behind just tightly enough to be comfortable and secure.

'Will this do?' I asked.

'Just check in the mirror. What does the mirror say?'

I looked in the mirror. But all I saw was myself, exactly that, just the same. I didn't look a bit like Thought Doctor or even like Fellow Traveller.

'All I see is myself, unchanged,' I said, somewhat disappointed.

'Exactly that,' said Fellow Traveller.' The journey was yourself, so it follows that the journey leads to yourself. And your Crown celebrates yourself.'

'Is that going to be alright, do you think?'

'That's the only way it *would* be alright. I think you are ready to submit your Crown to the Club,' said Fellow Traveller.

And together we walked towards the gates of the station at the end of the mountain path, both of us with heads high, wearing our Laurel Crowns.

Creating critical mass and momentum – how is this achieved?

Jackson (2000: p. 147) creates the starting point for this chapter in the process of initiating change in the organization by making an obvious but important point. He says: 'A vision that is not enacted upon is a dream. Building the framework for change starts the process of change, but now it has to be acted upon. The first step is to communicate the vision to the whole organisation.'

To bring about change in any organization is not an easy task. It was recognized earlier in the book that most if not all people have a degree of reticence, reserve or even opposition to the notion of change. It disturbs the status quo of the individual and the organization, and for those who were or will be affected, it removes the comfort zone in which they exist.

So far in the book we have examined the creation of the desired culture, shared the development of the vision for the organization and established the leadership framework judged by the leadership team to be the most appropriate vehicle to deliver the vision.

So what next?

The simplistic response is to communicate intent and action to the whole of the organization. This is particularly relevant when, as in Chapter 4, the concept of collegiality was one of the end goals. Everyone in 'the team' needs to be pulling in the same direction with a clear view of the end product. The concept of full and in-depth communication with all involved is of paramount importance. Jackson (2000) is of the firm belief that stress, misunderstanding and reticence can be overcome by clear communication. He makes the point that all members of any organization have their own set of standards, beliefs and interpretations of what is being proposed. This understanding will be culled from their personal experiences and understandings of the organization. In addition it will depend on their position in the organization and the degree to which they were consulted or involved in the change making plans and processes. Because each individual has this 'belief set' imprinted in their psyche, it is vitally important for the leadership team to appreciate the need for clarity of communication. Individuals will be, and are, selective in what they hear and how they hear it. Consequently, messages can be misunderstood, misconstrued or mischievously misinterpreted. Many a doubting Thomas will be happy to put up opposition on the back of misinterpretation, the cynics and unbelievers will be happy to use the selected information to act as a weapon against the proposed change. The compliant will be pacified and become enthusiastic with the provision of fulsome doses of facts.

It is the personal selectivity of the information which is the most difficult to overcome. That is why it is crucial for the organization's leaders to have thought through all the implications of the proposed change well in advance of publication. This alone will not suffice however. This is the starting point not the end. The starting point is the consistent provision of quality information regarding the project. This has then to be supplemented by what Jackson (2000) calls *communiaction*: 'The only meaningful form of communication is communi-action, with the emphasis on action. People who are meaningfully involved in something take time to understand it' (p. 147).

It is the understanding of what is being proposed which is as important as the actions which follow. A factor such as communiaction is an extended version of the concept of collegiality addressed in Chapter 4. It implies active involvement in the process. Collegiality is also a sharing activity but is subtly different in both its actions and its outcomes. Our interpretation of Jackson's communiaction is that each and every member of the group is involved in direct activity. Collegiality is a term which embraces contributions from all and actions from some depending on the nature of the tasks identified and to be completed. The spirit of both terms is important. The group is involved in the change process. If a sense of collegiality prevails within the organization then the sharing and contributing of ideas becomes the norm. Individuals will contribute because they both understand and feel part of the processes of planning and subsequently of implementation. A collegial approach to change supports the best possibility of acceptance by the organization and the individuals within it. Simon Emery of Crown Lift Trucks makes the point that in his organization, 'no one has the monopoly on good ideas' so he is open to ideas and suggestions from anyone in the organization.

The initiation of the change process

We are now in a position to see the 'ball of change' start to roll. To achieve the 'critical mass' of support for a new initiative is a crucial step for the implementers of the proposed change. The size of the critical mass necessary to bring about change is the indeterminate and variable number of individuals which will differ from organization to organization, and sometimes within organizations differ depending on the nature and complexity of the change. The crucial factors in terms of numbers are dictated by the combination of the individuals involved. That is, who makes up the group in terms of standing and respect within the organization, how influential individuals are within the group, how convincing their orations and persuasive powers are and perhaps most importantly, how significantly the proposed change will affect the life and well-being of the individuals concerned. The closer the issues are to affecting the personal situation of the individuals, the more focused the arguments and feelings in support for or against become.

Transparency

To achieve the critical mass of agreement and cooperation, the benefits for the individual, the group and the organization have to be made crystal clear. Clear, concise, transparent arguments based on objective facts laid out in an understandable and logical manner located in the core business of the organization is the way to achieve congruency. This is persuasively achieved by using strategies outlined in Chapter 5 and the real power is to harness the strength of the group to persuade the 'doubters'.

Transparency must be supported at every stage by the constant re-statement of the organization's mission, goals and targets and direction. Syngenta undertook this process by using their companies 'spine diagram' referred to as Figure 2.1 in Chapter 2. Chime do it by constant referral to the aims using multimedia approaches throughout the parent company and the 30 satellite companies on a weekly basis. St John's have started the process by using the structure diagram Figure 1.5 but have some way to go. A positive approach undertaken by Mitsubishi Heavy Industries is noted in Jackson (1997).

This organization established a clear mission statement which they took the opportunity to display as often as possible. They called it the 'Pentagon Campaign'. In Figure 6.1 the left hand chart shows the mission statement featured prominently at its head. This is followed by the five *Critical Success Factors* (CSFs) identified by the company for that particular year and relevant to their organizations goals and targets. In addition to the CSFs, the company also identified *benchmarks* from leading world competitors in the same field for each of the success factors.

Superimposed on this annually were the company's targets for that year for each benchmark, the companies' overall performance and the actual results attained as lines inside the pentagon in different colours. This was then individualized for each section throughout the organization, printed and displayed in every section area and work place. Each section of the company could then see how they were performing relative to other sections, relative to the company as a whole which was then measured against the international benchmarks. Using this information, each worker is in no doubt as to the progress of the company at section and company level. On the right hand side of the chart are hand written entries identified as team agreed activities which would specifically contribute to the overall aim of the company. This list is then easily crossed referenced with the stated aims and mission of the company making it transparent to all.

These targets are updated on a regular basis as each team successfully completes and attains the targets it sets itself. The Japanese call this *visible management* (Jackson

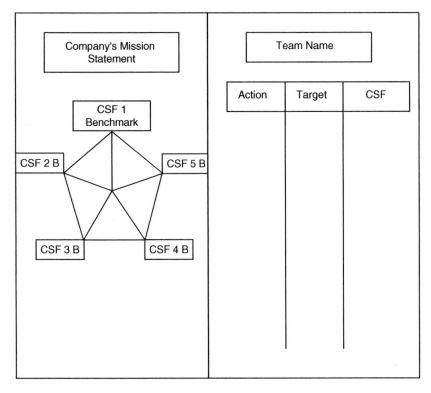

Key: CSF = Critical Success Factors for the company

B = Benchmark : Company's targets for the year measured on an international basis for each of the pentagon arms

Figure 6.1 Mitsubishi Heavy Industries – Pentagon Campaign

1997: p. 85) and it is one way of ensuring that the mission of the organization, the goals and targets at team, section, group and organization level are known, understood and created collegially by the organization. It helps to unite the workforce while allowing, individuals, groups, teams or sections to make their own plans and contributions to the overall direction of the company.

How was change achieved at St John's – a small case study

The aim of the change was to establish a new staffing structure and to introduce the concept of collegiality as a work practice.

Using St John's as a mini case study, it might be useful to see how one organization tackled the process of implementing change. As recorded in previous chapters, the germ of the idea originated from the Headteacher several years before it became public knowledge, and the Strategic Leadership Team spent many hours shaping the model of change to fit the specific needs of the school, before going public to the workforce.

There were two tiers of factors to be considered affecting this change process. The first tier was the statutory need to restructure under the government's TLR guidelines and at the same time enable the structure to accommodate the change in the teaching and learning strategies. A second tier was a longer term need to plan for the school's single site rebuild in five years time. This seems like a distraction to the initiative, but the rationale was trying to remove the need for a second tranche of change later in the life of the school.

On a theoretical basis, using Lippitt et al. (1978) categorization of change strategies, this was in part an *adoptive change* in as much as the motivation for the change was from external pressure, initially 'top down' in approach and motivated by an authority figure, in this case the Headteacher. This approach is described by Lippitt et al. (1978: p. 24) in the following way; 'The aim [is] to get the client to change in certain specific ways, to adopt certain practices, [and to] use certain technological devices.' The Headteacher had a very strongly held and clear personal educational philosophy which was ground breaking in its concept. There were no models on which to base the structure so it had to be a top down authoritative approach. It justifies its 'adoptive' label because the external motivating pressure was initially from the introduction of the TLR framework. The change also needed to encompass and be sensitive to the individual school, its local context, culture and ethos that the school has developed. In doing this it was also part of Lippitt et al. (1978) 'adaptive change' concept. The whole change process quickly fell under the embracing actions of collegiality as the introduction process unrolled.

One of the early precepts that the SLT recognized was that in the restructuring process, the existing roles and post holders had to be divorced from thoughts for the new structure. The discussions had to focus on what the new structure needed and the type of individual who may fulfil that role. Once those parameters had been established, the existing workforce could be considered. Inevitably, there were bound to be mismatches. This had two facets to it. The positive facet was that it gave both the school and the individual teacher's opportunities for career development, promotion and progress. The down side was that there were individual personal concerns about loss of status, pay levels and positions.

Having formulated the strategy, and established the leadership model that suited the school, the next and in many ways most significant step was to appoint a set of new teaching posts called Directors of Teaching and Learning. Appointees were to be experienced teachers who would be responsible for the Curriculum Schools. Curriculum Schools were subject areas grouped together because of similarities in the skills required or concept interrelationships between them. For example, the Curriculum School of Human Exploration contained the subjects Mathematics, Science, Earth Sciences and Psychology. The Directors of Teaching and Learning would be the catalyst for activities that took place in the Curriculum Schools, but not necessarily the leader in the true collegiate sense. The leader for a particular task was to emerge as the individual with the most appropriate skills or experience best suited to the task in hand. With the leadership framework appointed, established and briefed, the public phase of the revelation could then be undertaken.

The leadership task was to bring the plan to the attention of the workforce. All employees had previously been involved in the re-formulation of the aims and mission statement and so were already part of the development process of revamping the image of the school. The process started with a full staff meeting for all employees, teaching and support staff, at which the general structure was outlined by the Headteacher. These meeting all took place in the spring of 2005 and the time scale set externally by the DfES was that all TLR posts had to be in place by January 2006. The new structure was completely different from the previous conventional organization for a school and involved a completely different approach to all processes involved in the life of the school. In addition, there was a bank of new posts with new roles and titles associated with them. The first meeting ended in a stunned silence while everyone tried to take in what had been explained to them. Then slowly the questions started to come. As might be expected, they all revolved around the 'How does this affect me and my career' concerns. The Strategic Leadership Team had been thoroughly briefed and was conversant with the responses to these anticipated questions. As a team, they shared the responses in the public meeting. This did two things strategically; first it answered the personal questions from the staff. Secondly it showed the confidence, support and understanding the leadership team had for the Headteacher and the new ideas. Once the initial questions were answered, the different teams that made up the structure then dispersed to discuss the new ideas. These were then sent to the Headteacher and the opportunity was also made available for individuals to approach the Headteacher if they felt the need for more information.

A week later, another meeting was called to feed back on the queries raised. Towards the end of this meeting, the workforce was divided into two groups, the teachers and the support staff. This was done intentionally because the TLR changes, and changes to teaching methodology and the curriculum only involved the teachers. The support staff, led by the Bursar, were able to further investigate the changes in their own forums. The idea was that they were informed and included in the discussion, but as the process was to have little effect on them and their work practices they were not required to do anything else. This was a mistake, and its effects will be discussed later in the chapter.

The next set of meetings was held in the new team groupings. A Director of Teaching and Learning led the meeting initially, but led in such a way that a natural order grew organically with team members taking on roles as they became apparent during the discussions. This became a major hurdle for the successful implementation of the structure and will be discussed later.

An expected outcome from these discussions was that individuals began to identify themselves with the new roles and this in turn raised issues. Quite clearly, some roles transferred from the existing structure to the new roles, others clearly did not. The Headteacher had made it clear that under the TLR guidelines, no member of the teaching staff would lose pay as a result of the changes. However this 'ring fencing' of pay levels was to be held for three years after which the protection would stop and the posts disappear. This provoked considerable discussion and some heartache. During the Summer Term 2005 the new teams met on a regular basis to establish working patterns and responsibilities. During this time, some difficulties started to emerge.

Some hurdles that were experienced and how they were overcome

This process was not entirely smooth, and it is worth considering the problems which emerged and how the leadership and the school overcame them.

Post and role confusion

 As identified already, the new post names and specifications were confusing for most of the staff because there were no parallels in conventionally structured schools. Most teachers know what a Head of Department does, and what the responsibilities are for that post. New titles and specifications such as Director of Impact and Innovation needed in-depth explanation to help with the understanding. Although job descriptions were available for each of the new posts, staff either could not or would not fully understand them initially which led in turn to resentment, some obstruction and some lowering of moral. The Strategic Team worked very hard and continuously using a variety of media approaches and team meetings to dispel fears and to demonstrate how individual posts fitted into the big picture.

Promotion prospects

Later on in the implementation process, the new names and posts had a second cause for concern. The concern arose when teachers were applying elsewhere for promotion and change to other schools. How did these new posts equate with posts in more traditionally organized schools. The promotion difficulty was overcome by the Headteacher and Deputy Headteacher ensuring that when writing references for colleagues applying for posts in other schools that the appropriate skill sets of the individuals making the application met with the requirement on the application form.

Redundant staff in the new structure

All posts in the new structure were available for application from all staff. The posts were advertised internally together with the job descriptions and staff were invited to apply. It had already been agreed by the SLT prior to advertisement that interviews would be held for all likely candidates. This turned out to be a wise and significant safeguard for the Headteacher and his team. Those colleagues who applied but did not have the expertise or experience were seen individually by the Headteacher who suggested appropriate professional development avenues to them to aid future applications. As the appointment process unrolled and posts were filled, it became obvious that there would be few colleagues who needed to make some career decisions. They could stay in the posts that they held, understanding that the post would disappear in three years time together with the salary for that post, or change, adapt and apply for posts that required different skills which may be out of their comfort zone initially. The third option was to move schools before the new structure was set firmly in place. Surprisingly, there were one or two staff who did not seem able or willing to appreciate the implications that were spelt out for them and made no move either to apply for posts in other schools or to change career direction within St John's. The SLT could only continue to point out the end situation to them, offer continuing professional development opportunities and career counselling.

Promotion jealousies

All the new posts were available to any member of the teaching staff who felt they had the necessary skills and experience to fulfil the requirements of the job specifications. This was like a breath of fresh air to the school because it moved the logjam of sitting tenants who were not now efficient, but were not prepared to move. Inevitably, some colleagues were appointed to new and often promoted positions over more experienced or older staff. This tended to cause some resentment at first, but as the process was transparent and open the disillusioned and malcontents had only themselves to blame if they did not make application for the posts in the competitive arena of interviews. From the schools point of view, the change of personnel reinvigorated the whole system and enabled very motivated staff with new ideas and enthusiasm to take the school forward in a new direction.

Lack of clarity in the new roles and the implications for them

A major hurdle for the implementation of the new structure and the teaching and learning outcomes was an apparent lack of clarity about what was envisioned for the new roles. Colleagues were not initially able to transfer from their previous experiences to the new proposed way of working. As a consequence, there was great unease and concern as to how it all fitted together. To add to this, there was resistance to adopt a collegial approach to problem solving which particularly affected the ex-Heads of Department. Previously they had seen themselves as managers of their subject area, not specifically just leaders. There is comfort in managing because to is prescribed and has clear parameters. Once that management role was transferred to others, the Heads of Department, now re-rolled as Directors of Impact and Innovation were released to undertake leadership and visionary activities. This was not just for their subject area, but for the whole curriculum school for which they were responsible. This proved to be a step too far for some teachers in the early days of the implementation. The remedial actions were of support, encouragement and clear communication by the leadership team to enable this group of staff to establish themselves with confidence in their new roles.

A lack of a collegiate approach within the new structure

Associated with the new staffing structure for the school was the new collegial approach as outlined in Chapter 4. While many teachers would argue that they have always adopted a collegial approach to their professional duties, their practice would often belie that. True collegiality does not come naturally to all, particularly when status or pay is added to the equation. For the more forceful or ambitious members of any group or team, it is quite difficult to step back and let someone else take the lead even if they are better qualified to do so. It is equally hard for the more reticent to volunteer their services even if they are best suited to the task in front of more experienced and respected colleagues. So there became a stagnation of activity. Some argued that others in the team were paid more or had more time than them so they should be picking up all the necessary tasks and doing them. Others were just lazy and allowed other to pick up tasks so that they could enjoy and easier life. Others plainly just could not see what needed to be done.

Collegiality got off to a shaky start with the teams. The Headteacher adopted an intentional 'hands off' approach at the start to give teams the opportunity to develop as teams and to allow them to identify allocate and carry out the necessary tasks associated with their teams in their own individual way. This had mixed success in the early stages. What the Headteacher did do as a considered intent was to introduce a 'Trojan Horse' into the organization. This concept was outlined in Chapter 5 and the Trojan horse in the teams was the creation of posts called Phase Progression Leaders (PPLs). These teachers were recruited from a pool of very experienced staff in the school, many of whom had previously been conventional Heads of Year. The intention with the new posts was to remove the pastoral care of the students and allocate that to another group of people. Then to use the experience and expertise of the newly appointed Phase

Progression Leaders to maintain the learning progression of the students as they moved from one key stage to the next in their journey through the school. On the surface this appeared to be a relatively simple leadership task but as colleagues interrogated the role further, the Trojan horse began to emerge. During development, it became obvious slowly that this group of teachers were a corner stone of all that happens in terms of teaching and learning. As teams asked who should be doing this or that task, it became obvious that this group of staff were the ones with the expertise and experience in the area. It became clear that this team of staff had to have powers of persuasion, ability to delegate, vision, and respect from their peers and experience in order to undertake their role. It was this group of people who initially seemed to be the most put out by the changes that were being suggested. As time and discussion moved on, they began to use their expertise and experience and started to identify what needed to be done and by whom. They became some of the natural leaders in the collegiate groups. Their motivation grew with their involvement and they were in the end one of the main driving forces from within the staff.

The self-appointed ambitious but inappropriate leader

This was a small hurdle that appeared in a few of the teams during the change process. Confident, ambitious but sometimes inappropriate leaders will sometimes emerge; self appoint and hog the proceedings. They often do this to try and impress, gain respect or bully the group to their way of thinking in order to achieve some personal end. If this is not addressed quickly by other strong members of the group, this can lead to resentment and negativity from the team which is clearly counterproductive.

Cynics

It is perhaps inevitable when any change take place, that there will be a percentage of the workforce for a variety of reasons who will not embrace the change in a positive way, and a smaller but significant percentage who will cynically try to disrupt or disturb the change process. Analysis of the motives for this cynicism is varied and complicated. Some do not like change because it has a perceived effect on them financially, or in terms of status. Others do not have the intellectual ability to fully comprehend the significance of the change and are unable to see the longer term benefits. Others feel passed over for promotion by younger or less experienced colleagues. Whatever the reason, this small group of individuals often try to upset the smooth implementation of change. The Headteacher and Strategic Leadership Team were able to quickly identify these cynics and diffuse the situation to a certain extent by individual counselling and direct personal conversations. However, the insidious nature of a cynical undercurrent is difficult to dispel completely. Two years on, Bosher (2008) was still able to identify the presence of cynics on the staff and measure the effect that they were having on the activities. This had reduced from the previous survey by Wyse (2006) but still remained a potent force to be managed. It is particularly dangerous for the successful implementation of any project because cynics can have a very influential effect on the young inexperienced or easily influenced members of the workforce. This is so particularly if the cynical voice is that of an experienced colleague with status in the school.

Decision making permissions

This hurdle may seem a strange one to note, but it provided quite a problem for the Strategic Leadership Team. Collegiality and radical collegiality within the teaching teams slowly took off as more staff became a) more able to understand the concept and its implications, and b) became more confident and prepared to be accountable for their actions. From the start of the change process, the Headteacher had been trying to instil a feeling of confidence in all his staff in terms of accountability, decision making and decision taking. Permission to take and make decisions was given to all, together with the individual accountability responsibility that goes with that power. For some, taking decisions was a true release of delegated power to them which they embraced effectively and with enthusiasm. For many, taking responsibility and being at the front of the decision making process made than feel insecure and uncomfortable, others were not able to do it at all. The Headteacher on many occasions re-confirmed his support and confidence in his staff to make the right decision at the right time. He supported this with his assurance of support if mistakes were made. A difficulty that arose was that a small number of decision takers made a classic mistake. They did not inform the Headteacher of the decisions they had taken without consultation with him. Sometimes these were significant decisions with financial implications and if they affected the operation of the school and involved outside agencies such as the parent body occasionally caused problems. When this occurred the Headteacher discussed the issue with the individual or individuals concerned so that an appropriate protocol for decision making and taking was re-established.

Hind sight is a wonderful thing – mistakes that were made and what would have been a better approach

During the implementation of change in the school, some mistakes were made and with the clarity of hind sight would not be repeated again.

1. The first mistake was the lack of clarity in explaining in greater detail to all the staff the proposed changes, the implications for the school and the implications for the individuals in the workforce.
2. Mistake two was not having a schematic diagram available at the outset to enable the entire workforce to fully appreciate the interrelationship between different facets of the new structures.
3. More time should have been given to the development of the concept of collegiality in the existing structure before confronting the workforce with it at the same time as they were struggling with new job titles and responsibilities.
4. All the support staff workforce should have been involved in the collegiality process and embraced into the new structure at the same time as the teaching staff. Bosher (2008) discovered that even after two years of operation, there was still a seething discontent for their position at the workplace.
5. The governing body needed to be as well informed of the various interrelationships as the teaching staff in order to support the Headteacher and his staff in their work. Two years later there were still some pockets of misunderstanding.
6. The student body and parents should have been more involved in the process even if it did not directly affect them. They should have been consulted and given a 'voice' (Bosher 2008).

Hindsight is a wonderful gift, and it has to be recognized that the changes that were brought about in the institution were done so for a structure that had not been tried before. Wisdom comes with experience, and so it was with these changes. Many could not be foreseen, but because there were rigorous quality control processes in place and responsible SLT, appropriate changes could be made swiftly.

The process of change will manifest itself with many of the characteristics noted above in any organization. While the specific problems identified with St John's are just that, specific, other in-house problems of a similar nature will occur in other organizations. The message from this chapter is to plan thoroughly, communicate clearly and in great detail. Understand the problems and anxieties from the employee's point of view and encourage participation whenever possible. *Communi-action* (Jackson 2000) is the key to success. Finally, make sure that there are rigorous quality assurance processes in place and the client base is surveyed regularly. David Jackson made the point in conversation that 'Every organisation is perfectly designed to get the results that it does'. This truism is dangerous ground for the complacent organization. The head of the organization has a duty to make sure that his or her organization is designed to get the results that it needs, and is sufficiently flexible and sensitive enough to change direction or approach if the required end is not being achieved.

Collegiality is not the sole preserve or property of St John's School. The power of a collegiate approach to leadership is now becoming a global methodology. The next chapter will introduce the concept of global collegiality, not just as another tool of leadership, but as an essential leadership strategy to take organisations forwards into the twenty-first century.

7 Collegiality in a global context

In the world of education change is an ever present phenomenon. It is a response to dissatisfaction with the construct of the moment, to a target-led regime that demands and sets ever higher and more challenging targets and to a world that is changing more rapidly than at any time in its history. There seems to be a tension constantly operating between the values and practices of the past and the uncertainty of the future.

Independent school education thrives in the UK and the USA, suggesting dissatisfaction with the state education system. In most cases the independent sectors reinforce educational and social traditions that could be considered a 'throw back in time'. This does not imply criticism but highlights the importance that traditional approaches to education have in the minds of many. The pre-eminence of schools such as Eton, Harrow, Wellington and Marlborough College is guaranteed by the stable, unchanging ethos emphasizing tradition and students educated for a particular socio-economic client group. This concept of what a 'good school' looks like/feels like is bound to the mists of time but also the prosperity of the present. 'Successful' state schools, particularly selective state schools, tend to ape the independent school ethos in terms of uniform, rituals and teaching pedagogy.

Leadership also falls into the 'old' hierarchical structure in most independent schools and those that aspire to be like them. After all change is a threat to the financial stability of the school and the intertwined perceptions of its customers. A militaristic structure of leadership guarantees that the status quo will remain and boarders with new ideas (i.e. those that threaten the ethos) will be repelled.

It could be argued that these organizations do not get the best out of their human resource and yet the indisputable fact is that they are successful, achieve highly and 'get the results'. This often equates to high exam pass rates, successful admission to prestigious universities and consequently, through the public school network, success in life. There is a subtle matter of selection that is also pertinent but this is a distraction from the central issue which is that the 'elite' schools represent the bastion of tradition.

For a world facing considerable challenges of sustainability in terms of resources, climactic catastrophe and conflict, the old way will not be sufficient. In earlier chapters the development of the curriculum towards creating capable, confident learners who see no limits to what they can accomplish was explored. Over a period of eight years since its inception in 2000–2001, the Opening Minds Curriculum has done literally that. Not only did the curriculum approach open minds for the children, it opened the doorway for challenging the relevance of the restrictive national curriculum at Key Stage 3 (the first three years of secondary education). From a small beginning (six schools) the approach broadened and evolved as many teachers, and some brave Headteachers, adopted the principles of the new curriculum. Such was the weight of feeling that this was an approach more appropriate to the twenty-first century learner that central government finally loosened the strictures of the statutory curriculum to allow for adoption of learner-centred approaches.

National influence begins a process of change it does not signal that the end has been reached. As the seeds of change are sown, signs of strong growth begin to appear. In the Government's new Academy programme the RSA raised two million pounds in sponsorship to build the RSA Academy in Tipton, West Midlands. Designated to commence full operation in 2010, the Academy will be a flagship for the Opening Minds approach. Several hundred schools have adopted approaches aligned with Opening Minds. In itself this is not enough. If real lasting change is to be wrought then it cannot simply be nation centric. All children everywhere have the right to an education that will prepare them to take the human race on to the next level in human development and aspiration. In many countries, for example, China, Korea, India the pedagogical approach to learning is reminiscent of late nineteenth century/early twentieth century Britain. Learning by rote rather than for understanding and high expectation focused towards the labour market of emerging economies, produces education with a different value system. Education is highly valued, its importance is paramount and yet its purpose is not aligned with the needs of the learner but rather the state.

Where educators have slightly higher degrees of freedom, the passion to create a curriculum and an approach to learning that will catapult children forward to being prepared for the uncertainties ahead, is there in abundance. Emerging from the Opening Minds work the practice of restricting the approach to national boundaries was explored alongside the potential to globalize the approach. Coincidentally the European Commission in the Lisbon summit of 2004 determined that a competency based approach to the curriculum should be in place across member states by 2010. In 2007 that remained known to only a select few! The RSA with St John's and the RSA Academy began to develop the concept of a European Curriculum for the twenty-first century. The guiding principle behind the development was a recognition that learning to learn and key competencies embedded in the curriculum experience of every child, irrespective of birthplace, was essential in futures planning. The project therefore sought to create a model that could be replicated across national boundaries. It would be managed with a fluid and integrated approach that avoided dominance by one group and recognized the equality of professional experience and contribution to creative, new ideas and approaches to learning. Through a number of discussions and presentations (Hazlewood 2008), including one to a group of 40 American educators visiting the University of Oxford who were extremely enthusiastic about the new approach, the reality of a European network of schools emerged. (The Americans were keen to be involved as the project evolved.) Rapid responses were received from Germany, Croatia, the Czech Republic, Hungary, Greece, Poland and Lithuania (although not part of the European Union). The geographical location of the respondents has a relevance. Emerging from the old Communist Iron Curtain regime, in need of dramatic social and economic regeneration and keen to fully participate in the enlarged European Community, the degree of empowerment required for all young citizens is critical to achieving both progress and full participative partnership, sooner not later. Each country committed four schools and a University partner institution to the project. What becomes evident through this development of multi-national networks is that the old order, the traditional approach is no longer sufficient. The future demands something different.

The 'Developing Global Schools for the 21st Century Project' (DGS-21C as it became known) has a clear aim to identify ways of developing in young people the skills and aptitudes to function effectively as global citizens. The project intends to create opportunities to share learning experiences across national boundaries. Using cross-curricula and multi-disciplinary themes to explore similarities and differences in culture and life experiences the project focuses on what makes us (humans) unique, celebrates diversity and building the future as central themes. By creating narratives of personal learning around their lives, experiences and communities the hope is that enduring relationships are created at a professional and personal level that encourage a shared vision of building a future together.

DGS-21C has a wider agenda to develop a deep understanding of learning through an exponential approach between students and teachers on a transnational basis. It envisages teachers engaging on a number of levels, sharing pedagogies and practices, leading to the development of transnational units of learning for both teachers and students. The challenge to perception and practice is very considerable but the challenge to leadership of the project is even greater. International partnership is, by definition, a collegiate partnership. Equals coming together with common purpose searching for a way to transform the educational life chances of our students and therefore the planet.

It is on this point that the interface between education, educational leadership, business sector leadership and future scenarios begin to merge. The one thing that all commentators and analysts on the future can agree on is that the future is uncertain and unpredictable. Current evidence makes futures studies a compelling but quite frightening activity. A snapshot view of certain aspects of future scenarios based on present day information gives a small window on what may be to come:

Question:	Will there be sufficient water for the human race in the future?
Evidence:	Water tables are falling on all continents. 40 per cent of the human race are on international watersheds and 70 per cent of available water is used for agriculture. Agricultural productivity is expanding rapidly.
Implications:	Large scale water treatment needs to be revolutionized, desalination must become a far more significant contribution to the water resource, household sanitation needs to be revolutionized, and efficient watering systems for large tree plantations will be needed. Population growth must be balanced against resource production. New methods in food production will be needed, for example, stem cells producing meat tissue without the need to create the animal.

This small, incomplete insight into a real future scenario fits into a hugely complex jigsaw that includes ethnic conflicts, terrorism, weapons of mass destruction through to new and re-emerging diseases and immune system failure. The flip side of course is that if these are future scenarios how do we combat or minimize them? Education, innovation and collaboration on a global scale are essential ingredients to avoid the unthinkable.

Alternative futures education helping children to develop both optimism and a sense of control or empowerment about their own futures and that of the planet is not a strong curricula feature. It should be. Education in its traditional sense of 'being done to' rather than 'owned by' the learner must change. Autonomy in decision making, acquiring the knowledge and information necessary to inform those decisions become essential aspects of any student's experience. Working collaboratively with others across and beyond subject boundaries, removing the concept of pre-determined knowledge (or 'this is the way it is – accept it' approach) and releasing creativity will be vital if the bleaker futures scenarios are to be avoided. Confident learners who have developed insights can change the world and alter the future from probable to preferred. However, if this is to happen the way in which we perceive leadership must also change. The old Chinese proverb returns, *when great leaders have done their work, the people said, 'we did it ourselves'!*

In 2007 the Department for Children, Families and Schools commissioned Futurelab to look at the future of education in 2025 and beyond. The aim of the Beyond Current Horizons (2007) programme was to help the education system to prepare for and respond to the challenges brought about by social and technological evolution. The revolution in organizational response to the use of space and time, creating new ways of working, adapting and refining systems of communication and re-learning human interaction processes has seen a huge shift in a very short time. Education cannot afford a long time lapse while it catches up with the needs of the world beyond school. The all-encompassing role played by information technology creating new challenges and possibilities on an almost daily basis is immense. Harrison (2007) identifies the fact that, 'many people are experiencing the blurring of boundaries between living, working and learning . . . mobile communications and global business practices mean that people are connected 24/365'.

Harrison explores the near future and the human construct around management of the personal, academic and professional options. The picture that emerges is highly complex and made more so by resource depletion competing with economic growth.

The problems surrounding effective use of space in buildings that are heavily under-utilized but costly to maintain, is but one small aspect of a world that will need significant re-assessment in the years to come. However for education has come the lag behind what the human race of tomorrow will need and what it is being prepared for is very considerable.

In his analysis of *Childhood – 2025 and beyond* Prost (2007) identifies six key trends in childhood:

- Demographics – ageing population
- Diversification of living conditions and life chances
- Plural socialization
- Surveillance and regulation
- Individualization, consumption, voice and choice
- Emerging technological supplements.

Demographics and the ageing population indicate that the combination of declining birth rate and increased life span will move resources away from children and towards older people (by 2025 the median age will increase from 26 today to 37 – more people will be over 60 than under 15). If we are not very clear about the future vision for the education of our young the future may be bleak indeed.

Prost (ibid.), in examining the global economic trend and the rising prosperity of China, India, Brazil, and others, considers that the division in children's life chances, apparent through the twentieth century may be changing. The picture is complex and is affected by economic factors, political manipulation, social change (e.g. reduction in nuclear families, rise in cohabitation outside marriage) and rapid increase in transnational migration creating new racially and ethnic subcultural groups within individual nation states.

The concept of plural socialization identifies the impact of new technologies on children's socialization. No longer is the family pre-eminent in the creation of value systems and norms but the child is a focus for multi-media impact. Allied to large amounts of time away from home in nurseries, crèches, schools and so on, the nature of socialization is creating a very different type of child to those of past decades. The importance of looking at the child as an individual, at every level, is therefore so much greater than hitherto.

Prost goes on to say that, 'the twentieth century has witnessed increased levels of institutional control over children' (surveillance). Compulsory schooling being incrementally increased both at the lower end and upper end (the English Government's target for post-16 numbers in education and going on to University has now increased significantly in the last ten years) after school clubs, extended schools initiatives, holiday play schemes continually pressure children into more and more structured activity constantly under surveillance.

Paradoxically the increased emphasis on personalization of the curriculum (individualization) creation of individual learning pathways, the student voice is encouraged. The Opening Minds intent to create independent learners, who can think for themselves and have confidence in their ability to make independent decisions, lives inside this framework but for schools not aligned to this thinking/approach there may exist a tension in which student disengagement could be an increased phenomenon. Individual autonomy is made possible by 'new' technologies. The information age ensures that mobile communication is readily available and therefore conflict with more restrictive, linear forms of control (e.g. schools) is inevitable. Gone are the days of passing notes around the class – today a text does the job far more effectively! Cyber-bullying is a major concern and possibly what becomes reinforced is not transformation to autonomy but even greater reliance on a new subculture made possible by technology. Parental fears of the outside influence are considerably greater and yet the fear fuels the problem in that mobile phones are a 'must' (safety fears), in-house ICT is a 'given' (keeping them at home therefore safe) and yet the dichotomy is increased because many parents do not understand the language used or activity that the child engages in while 'online'.

Whichever way we look at it ICT wields enormous power and influence over every aspect of our lives. The boundary between education (school) and work (life beyond school) is now blurred – in a short time it may be non-existent. The rapid change in information and knowledge seems to be increasing exponentially. The underlying value system about what is worth knowing is also shifting. It does therefore raise questions around those who educate. If the target population is changing rapidly and perhaps the restrictions for learning are changing then how are the systems of education changing to adapt to the need of the moment and of the future?

Kress (2007) hits the mark when he states that any future view of education must incorporate a bridge between 'the processes active and valued outside the school and those processes active and valued inside the school'. While there are strong arguments for education in isolation as 'a good thing in its own right', there is a baseline of reality that recognizes that education is also crucial to the preparation of the individual for the working environment. Opening Minds (RSA 1999) emerged from an analysis of the world of work in the twenty-first century (RSA 1997) with the question, 'if that is what the world of work may look like, what will education look like?' Learning to learn, key competencies and skills are essential prerequisites in the preparation process. We have already stated that education has a vital role in determining the future in terms of scientific advancement and economic direction. In the era of globalization movement through different jobs in the average persons working life will be the norm. Therefore adaptability, flexibility and creativity will be core employer requirements. People who know how to learn to learn not simply for work but also for life will be highly valued assets.

It is an inescapable conclusion that if this change is to be managed then effective leadership at many levels will be essential. Most significant is the level of education in the compulsory and post compulsory education. It is not enough to consider local/national needs and leadership, a global revolution requires a global response and commitment. Teachers are, possibly by definition, a conservative group who can impede rapid change. Properly engaged they can be a force who propose and promote change. To achieve this the conditions need to be such that learning environments are created where all teachers are collaboratively involved in deep learning. Working *within* the school context is not sufficient. This new breed of proactive teacher focused on the needs of learners in the global economy must see connection and cooperation between schools nationally and internationally as an essential part of daily life. International cooperation at University level is well established and highly productive but in the earlier, formative phases 5–18 it is patchy and without a real plan. There are some excellent attempts to promote this approach, for example, the Specialist Schools and Academies Trust Inet programme, but it is an optional extra rather than an obligation. The Global Curriculum Project for the twenty-first century has potential but is working in a context that still sees national boundaries and socio-political directives as the determining factor. That may change but fear still exists for teachers and school Principals who step out into the limelight or emerge over the ramparts.

If the challenges identified by Futurelab are to be properly addressed in practice before 2025 then a revolution in management has to occur. This is much more likely to be on the education side rather than the business/economic sector side. The latter is well versed in survival and the need to embrace total employee engagement in the image reinvention game. The dinosaur is located within the sector that should be leading the charge through the perils of this century. If the dinosaur is to avoid playing a key role in the extinction process it must evolve rapidly.

The five challenges – beyond current horizons

Challenge 1 – generations and lifecourse
Understanding trends in demographics, family structure, intergenerational relationships and ageing.

Challenge 2 – identities, citizenship, communities
Understanding the development of cultural identity, citizenship and community in the context of globalising/localising forces.

Challenge 3 – knowledge, creativity and communication
Understanding trends in the creation, circulation and communication of knowledge.

Challenge 4 – work and employment
Understanding trends in work and employment.

Challenge 5 – state/market/third sector
Understanding trends in relationships between state, private and third sector provision of public services. (Futurelab 2008)

To evolve, the educational community must have a clear vision, an agreed set of values, a common purpose and one that is shared by all. This will demand strong, purposeful and resilient relationships that share the concept of equal professional status and equal personal and professional responsibility. The Tasmanian Government's Curricula Review (2004) identified the values of connectedness, resilience, achievement, creativity, integrity, responsibility and equity as the core for future school development. The Tasmanian Colleges identified four further values as identity, autonomy, diversity and flexibility.

In a searching analysis of person centred learning communities Fielding (2007) proposes that these communities are shaped around wider human purposes. Such schools:

- deliberately develop more participatory forms of engagement and decision-making,

- do not distinguish between pastoral and academic aspects of the school,
- embrace explicitly dialogic, even narrative,
- forms of continuing professional development, such as action learning sets and self-managed learning groups,
- dissolve boundaries between status, role and function through new forms of radical collegiality, such as students as researchers.

The person-centred learning we need will be:

- historical, because it understands the continuity of the past in the present
- substantial, because it attempts an explicit account of how we become persons
- connected, because it draws on intellectual and professional traditions from all around the world
- integrated, because it takes ethical, social, political and educational considerations into account
- positively troubling, because it is willing to rethink the wider social and political system in which we find ourselves
- social, because it takes into account the claims of wider social allegiance and the common good
- modest, because it avoids hyperbole and cliché
- meaningful, because it recognizes the importance of making meaning of our lives
- values-led, because it returns us to purposes and the way they inform processes
- intellectually informed, because it takes into account learning from research and the traditions of intellectual enquiry.

Underpinning Fielding's proposal is the presence of collegiality, ambiguity and openness as opposed to contract, clarity and closure. Fielding identifies the problematic conditions this creates for leadership suggesting that, 'those who run schools should not expect higher status than those who teach in it'. He goes on to state,

> the intellectual and practical legacy of both leadership and management has within it much of which we should be wary. Maybe the best we can do in the meantime is to legitimate that restlessness in ways which force us to ask hard questions, often in ways which are discomforting and problematic, and always in ways that take us back to fundamentals which should themselves be unsettled by a permanent provisionality born of lived experience and the felt necessity of care.

Among the 'hard questions' that need to be asked in the creation of a person-centred, future-focused learning environment are:

1. Do we have the will/courage to allow students to become full participants in the co-construction of the learning journey?
2. Has the concept of leadership moved sufficiently to accept that all who are re-employed to create effective learners have equal status?
3. Is the predominant hierarchical model stultifying student progression and creativity?
4. Are teachers being de-professionalized by an over-arching management structure that dis-empowers them – do they feel 'done to' rather than 'done with'?
5. Is the education of teachers and the continuing professional development of teachers sufficient or far reaching enough? Are they properly prepared to educate the next generation?
6. How long have we to go to get this right?

The last question is the most pressing. Bee populations in the USA are currently being devastated by an unidentified virus; as much as a third have been wiped out. Whether it is a virus, global warming, insecticides or, as is favoured at the present time, a fungus no one is quite sure. However, a quote probably mis-attributed to Einstein, postulates that, 'if the bee disappeared off the surface of the globe then man would only have four years of life left. No more bees, no more pollination . . . no more men'. This is more likely to have been the creation of European beekeepers during a political protest in 1994 over lower priced honey imports! However, the statement is compelling for the dramatic uncertainty that it conveys. The essence is crystal clear – there is little time to squander in bringing about a transformation to the way education is led and managed.

Cheng (2001) refers to the 'Triplization Process' in education reform and future educational development. The 'triple' are:

- Globalization which refers to the transfer, adaptation and development of values, knowledge, technology and behavioural norms across countries. The importance of educators seeing themselves as part of a global network, sharing intellectual resources and initiatives is crucial.
- Localization has the same components as globalization but focused on local contexts in which the adaptation of all related external values, initiatives and norms meet the local needs at the societal level.
- Individualization again contains the same components but at an individual level. The importance of individualization is in the generation of personal motivation, creativity and initiative.

Cheng's work emphasizes the student as the centre of learning. It contains the same basic precepts as Opening Minds.

Paradigm shift in learning

New Triplization Paradigm Individualized Student and Learning	*Traditional Site-Bound Paradigm* Reproduced Students and Learning
• student is centre of education • individualized programmes • self-learning with guidance • self-actualizing process • focus on how to learn • self-rewarding and enjoyable	• student is follower of teachers • standard programmes • absorbing knowledge from teacher • receiving process • focus on how to gain • externalized rewards
Localized, Globalized Students and Learning	School-Bounded Learning
• multiple local and global sources of learning • networked learning • lifelong and everywhere • unlimited opportunity • world class learning • local and international outlook	• teacher based learning • separated learning • fixed period and within school • limited opportunities • school bounded learning • school experiences

(Cheng 2001: p. 49)

The paradigm shift in learning demands a paradigm shift in teaching and in teacher education.

New Paradigm Individual Teacher and Teaching:	*Traditional Site-Bound Paradigm* Reproduced Teacher and Teaching:
• teacher is the facilitator to support students' learning • multiple intelligence teacher • individualized teaching style • teaching is to arouse curiosity • teaching is a process to initiate, facilitate, and sustain students' self-learning and self-actualization • sharing joy with students • teaching is a lifelong learning process	• teacher is the centre of education • partially competent teacher • standard teaching style • teaching is to transfer knowledge • teaching is a disciplinary, delivering, training, and socializing process • achieving standards in examinations • teaching is a transfer and application process

Localized and Globalized Teacher and Teaching:	School-Bounded Teacher and Teaching:
• multiple local and global sources of teaching and knowledge	• teacher as the sole source of teaching knowledge
• networked teaching	• separated teaching
• world-class teaching	• site-bounded teaching
• unlimited opportunities for teaching	• limited opportunities for teaching
• teacher with local and international outlook	• teacher with only school experiences
• as a world class and networked teacher	• as a school-bounded and separated teacher

Whichever way we look at the future, dramatic shifts are required. Cheng's paradigms are an excellent insight into where education needs to go but there is a huge problem. Many teachers in their 30s, certainly 40s and 50s, will find the mindset necessary to 'tripilize' the curriculum structure, create a world class and globalized curriculum and not least really individualize the curriculum, daunting to say the least. The complexity of 'pooling' world class resources through integrated networks of teachers worldwide, emphasizing global relevance in social, political, economic, technological and cultural terms is a tall order. For this group of teachers, the majority group, the necessary underpinning values and structures in teacher education are largely absent. Lifelong self-learning is not as sophisticated nor advances as it needs to be to revolutionize the learning context and environment. Waiting for the 'new generation' of teachers, wherever or whenever that may be, is not an option. Radical change calls for radical solutions.

Two of the other 'hard questions' that were not raised earlier were:

• will 'schools' continue to exist?
• do schools really need Heads/Principals?

It is probably important to address these first. In the future anywhere, anytime learning through ICT is highly possible but it would be a huge mistake to leap to the assumption 'therefore we don't need highly costly buildings called schools'. The social and interactive elements of learning, of people being together to establish the very essence of what it means to be human, requires a place for coming together. However, the old notion of school as a solitary place must change. Learning in the most appropriate environment whether it be real or virtual is important. At a local level, networks of schools/colleges offering specific courses, diplomas already operate very successfully sharing students and teachers. Local and international networks are essential. The logical extrapolation suggests that leadership can be shared across these networks, federations and clusters. The great strength that emerges from sharing pedagogy and knowledge, what Caldwell (2004) refers to as sagacity, goes some way towards Cheng's paradigm for both educators and learners. But do these schools and groups of schools need Heads/Principals?

In a truly collegiate organization all would be of equal status. The experience of St John's and its evolving 'management' structure is that collegiality does work but actually the structure never stands still. When *Heads* of Department, curriculum *leaders* are removed the questions start and the fears emerge. 'Who is responsible for X?' 'Who is going to do . . . ?' 'I don't know how to . . . ?' With careful coaching, guidance and sometimes a calming word, leaders emerge to take on a task, lead others through a problem and general support each other in 'getting the job done'. It removes the barriers that 'being in charge' places so effectively in the way of change and allows people from different parts of the organization, not always the most experienced or senior, to lead.

As the model has evolved very new and inexperienced teachers have taken on large scale initiatives with a great degree of success. They don't always succeed first time *but* they never fail. The team commitment to each other, the goals collectively set and the students always ensure that people pull together – not because they are told to but because they want to: the days of being de-professionalized by having professional autonomy subjugated to someone in authority have gone. What has emerged is an organic model of leadership and management, it is constantly changing as new priorities emerge and others diminish. Leaders emerge and change, but everyone knows and *believes* that they too can lead when the time is right.

It is an interesting dimension of social interaction and human nature that there will be those who don't want to lead , feel uncomfortable in that role or inadequate. This has proved not to be a factor at St John's. Collegiality emphasizes collective responsibility and professional integrity; not letting others down is a tangible part of the ethos. Rotation through roles is also a great strength. The days when the Head of English stayed in post gradually becoming a part of the scenery with all that longevity entails are also no longer. Role rotation allows others to gain experience at a younger age releasing their potential for enhanced leadership is a part of the organic leadership environment.

Being at the leadership edge can often be the sole desire of the Head/Principal and indeed that was the early experience of St John's in which the Head transformed the culture of the school by engaging with the Opening Minds Project. Since the introduction of the collegiate structure innovation and leading edge thinking has blossomed. The creation of a unique Virtual Learning Environment, involvement with curriculum development for the 2012 Olympics, DGS-21C, exemplary work in additional educational needs, a gifted and talented education, creativity and extended schools all bear testament to the rich potential unlocked by collegiality. These are but a few of many examples.

Embedded in this culture shift is the emergence of the student as co-constructor in their own learning journey. An example of St John's students engaging in the process is cited in Ritchie and Deakin-Crick (2007). The students as part of their learning journey participated in a university led research project around personalized learning. The premise in the research was that the choices that we make as individuals are direct reflections of who we are as human beings. One of the St John's students, Jonathan, saw the importance of the learner at the centre in these terms,

> It all ties together – it's about self awareness more than anything else . . . to chose your objects you need to understand yourself and your own story and you have to be self-aware . . . self-awareness is not even touched upon in the education system . . . part of the self-awareness thing is to tell your own story. (Deakin-Crick et al. 2007: p. 17)

The choice factor is important for every learner whether it be the student or the teacher. Clear visions for what can be achieved need to be a part of the dialogic in classroom interaction. Equally they must be part of the collegiate conversation. In creating an effective collegiate leadership (note *not* management) structure accessible to all participants things cannot be left to chance. A large group of people, students and teachers, rather like an orchestra, need a conductor. In terms of professional learning and development (PLD) at St John's this is done through a small committee comprised of teaching and non-teaching staff who are charged with examining the needs of the organization and individuals within it. Aware of the strategic plan, which all staff have had the opportunity to contribute to, the development priorities and performance management data, the committee determines the allocation of time and resource to PLD. Similarly other committees, some with limited remits others with a more longitudinal brief, orchestrate the development of the school. However, and answering one of the 'hard questions', an overall leader needs to keep the orchestra together! This leader needs to be both within the collegiate team and without. *Within* equals teaching, participating and contributing to the everyday aspects of school life. *Without* has two aspects: the first is the overview of the evolution of the organic model ensuring that growth is healthy, positive and aligned with the collective aspiration. Ever aware of the views and perspectives of students and teachers, sensitive to the *feel* of the organization. Intuitive understanding is a key part of collegiate growth – knowing when to act, when to stay quiet, when to quietly intervene. The second aspect is that of ambassador representing the collegiate aspiration, seeking new opportunities, identifying new partnerships, engaging with the sagacity of others in similar roles to create deepening pathways for learner development.

The interdependence so heavily emphasized in this model of leadership is fundamental. The co-dependency of collegiality expanding into strong localized and globalized partnerships ensures that learning will be challenging, demanding and intellectually rigorous. The creation of succession for new leaders is an integrated part of collegiality; those rising to the fore will be creative, energetic, emotionally intelligent, self-motivating and complete professionals. They in turn will know the power of collegiality to transform the learning journey into one where our preferred futures are realized.

References

APAPDC. (2004), *Learn, Lead, Succeed.*

Barry, D. (1991), Managing the bossless team: lessons in distributed leadership. *Organisational Dynamics* (1991), Vol. 21, No. 1, 31–47.

Bayliss, V. (1998), *Redefining Work.* London: RSA.

Bayliss, V., Brown, J., & James, L. (1998), *Redefining the Curriculum.* London: RSA.

Beyond Current Horizons. (2007), www.beyondcurrenthorizons.org. Accessed May 2008.

Bosher, M. A. (2001), *How can I as an Educator Working with Other Teachers Support and Enhance the Learning and Achievement of pupils?* Ph.D. Thesis. Bath University.

—(2008), *St John's School Marlborough: Evaluation of the Collegiate Management Structure; Continuation Phase.* Marlborough: St John's School.

Bosher, M. A., & Hazlewood, P. K. (eds) (2005*), Nurturing Independent Thinkers.* Stafford: Network Educational Press.

Boyle, B., While, D., & Boyle, T. (2004), A longitudinal study of teacher change: what makes professional development effective? In *The Curriculum Journal,* Vol. 15, No. 1, Spring 2004, Routledge.

Caldwell, B., & Spinks, J. (1988), *The Self Managing School.* Lewis: Falmer Press.

—(1998), *Beyond the Self Managing School.* London: Falmer Press.

Caldwell, B. (2004), *Re-imaging the Self-Managing School.* London: SSAT.

Carnegie Forum on Education and the Economy. (1986), *A Nation Prepared: Teachers for the Twenty-first Century.* New York: Carnegie Corporation of New York.

Cheng, Y. C. (2001), New education and new teacher education: a paradigm shift for the future. *Asia Pacific Journal of Teacher Education and Development,* Vol. 3, No. 1, 1–34.

Costen, P. (2007), Letter to the Daily Telegraph (2 October 2007).

Cruddas, L. (2007), '"Engaged Voices" – dialogic interaction and the construction of shared social meanings'. *Educational Action Research,* Vol. 15, No. 3, September 2007, 479–488.

Darling-Hammond, L., & Goodwin, L. A. (1993*),* Progress towards professionalism in teaching. In G. Cawelti (ed.) *Challenges and Achievements of American Education.* 1993 Yearbook of the Association for Supervision and Curriculum Development. Alexandria: Ventura Publisher 4.1.0.

Deakin,-Crick, R., Small, T., Milner, N., Pollard, K., Jaros, M., Leo, E. and Hearne, P. (2007), *Inquiring Minds: Transforming Potential through Personalised Learning,* London: RSA.

DES. (1977), *Ten Good Schools.* Department of Education and Science.

DfES. (2004), *School Workforce Reform.*

—(2004a), Every *Child Matters: Change for Children*. DfES/1081/2004.

—(2004b), *The Children Act*. 2004 London: HMSO.

Elmore, R. (1990), *Restructuring Schools*. Oakland: Jossey-Bass.

Fielding, M. (1999), Radical collegiality: affirming teaching as an inclusive professional practice. *Australian Educational Researcher*, Vol. 26, No. 2, August 1999.

—(2007), From personalised to person centred. *Raising Achievement Update* (October 2007).

Fullan, M., & Park, P. (1981), *Curriculum Implementation*. Toronto: Ontario Ministry of Education.

Futurelab. (2008), *Beyond Current Horizons Programme*. Bristol.

Goodlad, J. I. (1990), *Teachers for Our Nation's Schools*. San Francisco: Jossey-Bass.

Hakala, D. (2008), The ten top qualities of leadership. *HR World* 19 March 2008.

Handy, C. (1984), *The Future of Work*. London: Basil Blakewell.

—(1994), *The Empty Raincoat: Making Sense Out of the Future*. London: Hutchinson.

Hargreaves, A. (1991), Contrived collegiality: the micro-politics of teacher collaboration. In Blase, J. (ed.) *The Politics of Life in Schools*. California: Corwin Press.

—(1992), Cultures of teaching: a focus for change. In Hargreaves, A. & Fullan, M. (eds), *Understanding Teacher Development* . London: Cassell, 216–240.

Hargreaves, D. (2004), *Personalising Learning: Next Steps in Working Laterally*. London: SSAT.

—(2006), *Personalising Learning (6) the Final Gateway: School Design and Organisation*. London: SSAT.

Harris, A. (2004), Distributed leadership: leading or misleading. *Educational Management, Administration and Leadership*, Vol. 32, No. 1, 11–24.

Harrison, A. (2007), *Changing Spaces, Changing Places*: unpublished challenge paper. DEGW UK.

Haycock, K. (2007), *Education Leadership: A Bridge to School Reform*. Report on the Wallace Foundation 2007 National Conference. 25–32.

Hay McBer. (1998), *Models of Excellence for School Leadership*. NCSL.

Hazlewood, P. K. (1997), *The School Mission Statement*. School Prospectus.

—(2003), The RSA Opening Minds Competencies Curriculum: one school's attempt to raise standards by teaching children how to learn. *CSCS Journal*, Vol. 15, No. 1, Autumn 2003, 14–16.

—(2004), Opening Minds: education for the 21st century. *Teaching Expertise* 3, Spring 2004, 4–6.

—(2005), Making the news. In Bosher, M. A. & Hazlewood, P. K. (eds) (2005), *Nurturing Independent Thinkers*. Stafford: Network Educational Press.

—(2008), unpublished speech to the European Curriculum Network Group.

H. M. Government. (1998), *Teaching and Higher Education Act 1998*. London: HMSO.

Holt, J. (1965), *How Children Learn*. London : Penguin.

Hopkins, D., Ainscow, M., & West, M. (1994), *School Improvement in an Era of Change*. New York: Cassell plc.

Hopkins, D. (2005), *Leadership by Transforming Learning*. iNet Report: SSAT.

Hughes, E. C., Becker, H. S., & Geer, B. (1971), *Student Culture and Academic Effort*. in Cosin, B. R., Dale, I. R., Esland, G. M. & Swift, D. F. (1971), *School and Society: a sociological reader*. London: Routledge & Kegan Paul in association with The Open University Press.

Jackson, D. (1997), *Dynamic Organisations*. London: Macmillan Press Ltd.

—(2000), *Becoming Dynamic*. London: Macmillan Press Ltd.

Jones, A. (1987), *Leadership for Tomorrow's Schools*. In Hopkins, D., Ainscow, M. & West, M. (1996), *School Improvement in an Era of Change*. New York: Cassell plc.

Kark, R., & Van Dijk, D. (2007), Motivation to lead, motivation to follow: the role of the self regulatory focus in the leadership process. *Academy of Management Review* 2007, Vol. 32, No. 2, 500–528.

Kress, G. (2007), *New literacies, new democracies*: unpublished challenge paper. Centre for Multimodal Research, Institute of Education, University of London.

Lavié, J. M. (2006), Academic discourses in school based teacher collaboration: revisiting the arguments. *Educational Administration Quarterly*, Vol. 42, No. 5, 773–805.

Lawn, M., & Ozga, J. (1988), The education worker? a reassessment of teachers. In Ozga, J. (ed.) *Schoolwork: Approaches to the Labour Process of Teaching*. Milton Keynes: Open University Press, 81–98.

Lippitt, R., Hooyman, G., Sashkin, M., & Kaplin, J. (1978), *Resource Book for Planned Change*. Ann Arbor: Human Resource Development Association.

Lomax, P. (1999), *Coming to a better understanding of educative relations through learning from individual's representations of their action research*. Unpublished paper available from the author or at website http://kingston.ac.uk/~ed s477.

Lomax, P., & Whitehead, J. (1998), The process of improving learning in schools and universities through developing research-based professionalism and a dialectic of collaboration in teaching and teacher education. *Journal of In-service Education*, Vol. 24, No. 3, 447–467.

Marsh, D. (1997), *Educational Leadership in the 21ˢᵗ Century: Integrating Three Emerging Perspectives*. Paper presented to the Annual Meeting of the American Educational Research Association (Chicago 24–28 March, 1997).

McIver, C. (2006), *21st Century Educational Leadership: A discussion paper on the role of the Principal*. Tasmanian Department of Education. February 2006.

Murgatroyd, S., & Morgan, C. (1993), *Total Quality Management and the School*. Buckingham: Open University Press.

Murphy, J. (1991), *Restructuring Schools: Capturing and Assessing the Phenomena*. New York: Teachers College Press.

Nukerji, R. in Striker, S. (2003), *The Third Anti-Colouring Book* . New York: Henry Holt & Co. (First published 1980).

Ofsted. (2007), *Ofsted Survey Inspection Programme: Curriculum Innovation*. www.ofsted.gov.uk 28/02/2007.

Pearsall, J. (ed.) (1999), *The Concise Oxford Dictionary: 10th edition*. New York: Oxford University Press.

Prost, A. (2007), *Childhood – 2025 and Beyond*: unpublished challenge paper. University of Warwick.

Radice, B. (1971), *Who's Who in the Ancient World*. London: Anthony Blond (1971). Revised and published by Penguin (1973).

Rees, N. (1999), *Cassell Companion to Quotations*. London. Cassel.

Ritchie, R., & Deakin-Crick, R. (2007), *Distributing Leadership for Personalising Learning*. London: Continuum.

RSA (1997), *The World of Work in the 21ˢᵗ Century*. London: RSA.

—(1999), *Opening Minds: Education for the 21ˢᵗ Century.* London: RSA.

St John's School and Community College. (2005), *Inspection Report.* Ofsted.

Schein, E. (1984), Coming to a new awareness of organisational culture. *Sloan Management Review,* Vol. 25, No. 2, 3–16.

Scott, G. (1999), *Change Matters: making a difference in education and training.* Sydney: Allen and Unwin.

Smith, F. (1996), Leadership qualities. *Leadership Journal.* Fall 1996, Vol. 17, No. 4, 30.

Spiro, J. (2008), Eye and the Fellow Traveller Ph.D. epilogue University of Bath: available at http://www.jackwhitehead.com/monday/janeepilogue.htm /2007.

Stenhouse, L. (1975), *An Introduction to Curriculum Research and Development.* London: Heinemann.

Tasmanian Principals Association. (2004), *School leadership development paper.* TPA internal. Tasmanian Education Department.

The Holmes Group. (1986), *Tomorrow's Teachers.* East Lancing USA: The Holmes Group.

The Holy Bible. (1957), revised version in verses. Cambridge, London: Cambridge University Press.

West, M. (1994), *Effective Teamwork: Practical Lessons from Organisational Research.* Oxford: Wiley-Blackwell.

Wyse, B. (2006), St John's School and Community College Marlborough, an Evaluation of the Collegiate Management Structure: Preliminary Phase. St John's School.

Zuboff, S., & Maxmin, J. (2004), *The Support Economy.* New York: Penguin Books.

Index